MUSIC &
TECHNOLOGY

H.P. Newquist

Billboard Books
An imprint of Watson-Guptill Publications/New York

ABOUT THE AUTHOR

H. P. Newquist is a musician and writer whose articles have appeared in various music and computer magazines. He has been involved in numerous recording projects and currently operates a digital recording studio.

PHOTO CREDITS

Page 109 (Fig. 6–7), courtesy Akai Professional; page 143, courtesy Coda Music Software; page 18, courtesy Electronic Arts Foundation; page 79, courtesy Ensoniq; pages 106, 134 (Fig. 8–4), courtesy Russ Jones Marketing Group; page 78, courtesy Kurzweil Music Systems; page 76, courtesy New England Digital; pages 134 (Fig. 8–3), 145, courtesy Passport Designs; page 74, courtesy RolandCorp US; page 15, courtesy David Sarnoff Research Center; pages 21, 109 (Figure 6–8), Yamaha Corporation of America; page 73, photo by Studio V.

Copyright © 1989 by H.P. Newquist

First published 1989 by Billboard Books, an imprint of Watson-Guptill Publications, a division of Billboard Publications, Inc., 1515 Broadway, New York, NY 10036

Library of Congress Cataloging-in-Publication Data

Newquist, H. P. (Harvey P.)
    Music & technology / H.P. Newquist.
      p. cm.
    Includes index.
    ISBN 0-8230-7578-8
    1. Electronic music—History and criticism. 2. Music—Data processing. I. Title. II. Title: Music and technology.
ML74.N48   1989
780′.285—dc20
                                          89-9818
                                            CIP
                                            MN

Manufactured in the United States of America

First printing, 1989

1 2 3 4 5 6 7 8 9 / 94 93 92 91 90 89

Acknowledgments

There are many people that I wish to thank for the help, support, and assistance they provided during the course of this undertaking.

I most appreciatively would like to single out: Tracy Smith, agent extraordinaire; Tad Lathrop and Fred Weiler of Billboard, whose foresight, persistence, and early morning phone calls brought this book to reality.

Thanks to the individuals in the music and technology industries who shared their time, especially those at Roland, Alesis, BBE, Passport, Opcode, Yamaha, Coda Music Software, EAR Music, Music Maker Publications, Cherry Lane Music, TEAC, Computerworld, and AI Expert.

Certain people made sure that I always found music to be worth the effort. They are: Tucker Greco and family, Barbara Seerman, and also Neil Ferris.

Special thanks to John Gibson at EAR in Phoenix and Doedy Hunter at Apple Computer, without whom much of this information would never have seen the light of day; and to Tom Wojtas, who went with me into the MIDI jungle and helped me live to tell about it.

Thanks also to the teachers that made all the difference: John Kunkel, David Bernstein, and Professor Thomas Werge. Your efforts meant more than you'll ever know.

Credit is due to the residents of Skid Row at the University of Notre Dame, who put up with 3 A.M. experiments in guitar amplification; most especially to Mike and Barb Johnson, who provided me with a place to lay my laptop computer in the final hours of this writing; and to the Boys, Dan Collins and Tim Dunn, who still don't believe that I actually work for a living.

I am grateful to my father and mother, and to my brothers and sisters, Lee, Anne, Bob, Ed, Margi, Jim, and Mike. Without any of them, there would be no love of music, no guitar playing, no new music to be created, no lessons to be learned, and no book in front of you.

And thanks, of course, to Trini. Dreams are always just that—dreams —until someone gets you to chase them.

Contents

Introduction

Technology is an easy thing to deal with. Each of us encounters some form of modern technology every day, perhaps every waking hour. Telephones, microwaves, VCRs, new cars, calculators, stereos, televisions, and a host of other products are all examples of devices that we handle easily, without ever thinking twice about it.

Dealing with music technology should be the same way. That's the reason for this book.

Unfortunately, whenever you talk to other musicians about advances in music technology, their eyes tend to glaze over. I can't count the number of times I have been in music stores and listened to people try to understand the techno-babble that comes out of product literature and brochures. On paper, very little of it makes sense. It is like listening to somebody read a description of how airflow and dynamic pressure affect a wing-shaped object to make aircraft fly. Listening to it is not the same as experiencing it.

At the same time, answers to questions are too hard to come by. Practical working knowledge of how equipment works in real life, and not in the manual, seems almost nonexistent when people look for help. The usual answer one hears for a musician with a technical problem is "I don't know, man. Maybe you've got the thing plugged in the wrong place somewhere." *Wonderful* words of advice. That and 20 cents won't even buy you a Dr. Pepper. And it sure won't resolve your equipment problems.

There is really no one to blame for this state of affairs, however. Many of the people who work on the technical side of developing this software and equipment think that it's pretty obvious to everybody. This attitude also affects other technical people, like some math teachers. These people believe that since it's readily apparent to them, then it must be readily apparent to anyone they explain it to. I had a calculus teacher who used to yell when I couldn't understand certain concepts, "What do you mean you don't know what the percentage of increase of the cubic volume of air is in a hot-air balloon rising at 20 feet per second with an outside temperature of 60 degrees and an internal temperature of 140 degrees? It's as plain as the nose on your face! Are you saying you *still* don't understand?" That's exactly what I was saying. Needless to say, I didn't excel under this man's direction.

Most people who work in music stores are trying to figure this stuff out for themselves just like the rest of us, but they're also trying to sell it. They can't spend a lot of time helping to work out all of your problems while other customers wait. This is also true for company representatives who are constantly trying to understand a never-ending array of equipment produced by their own companies.

This book will hopefully get around some of the obstacles to making the technology work for you. Over the last few years, I have spent too many days and nights fighting with equipment, yelling at software, swearing at manuals, cursing at manufacturers, and weeping openly at cables plugged into the wrong place, trying to get all of these tools to work for my own musical projects. Much of what I learned from those days of frustration is contained in this book. There are three points worth noting that I have learned from all of this:

- All of this neat stuff works—once you get past the fancy terms and names—and helps create music at levels far above what most of us have known in the past.

- If it *doesn't* work, check it again. 90 percent of all the bitching and moaning I did learning this stuff was because I wasn't paying attention—I forgot to plug a cable back in, or set the proper MIDI channel, or even turn something on. You know how you feel when you get into someone else's car and you can't find the door handle or the headlight switch? It's there, all right; you just have to keep looking for it.

- Never *ever* give up. Persistence is going to make you the master of this stuff. It only takes a little bit of time once you get started. If you give up, you lose. And then they send you to technology hell, where even the light switches don't work without a 200-page manual.

Now that you've read that, and committed it to memory for the rest of your musical life, let me go over a couple of things about this book.

With regard to how quickly modern music technology changes, I've tried to keep the description of certain products as general as possible. Too often you'll read about a new and intriguing piece of music equipment, only to find out that the manufacturer *already* has a new and improved version available that you really know nothing about. Or you buy something recommended highly in a book or magazine, and two weeks later, something with more features comes out, and you feel as if you got stuck with last year's model.

For these reasons, I've tried to avoid mentioning specific manufacturers and specific products, focusing more on what products in a certain category can do and what makes them do it. Individual products come and go, but product categories do not. I do single out particular machines and manufacturers in the context of their historical significance.

While refraining from discussing specific products, I do want to acknowledge certain products that formed the basis for much of the information and examples I've used in the following chapters. They include the Apple Macintosh II personal computer; the Alesis HR-16 Drum Machine, as well as the Alesis Midiverb II Digital Effects Processor; Passport Designs' Master Tracks Pro Sequencing Software; Coda Music's Finale scoring software; Opcode's Software Editor/Librarians; BBE's Sonic Maximizer; the Roland GM-70/GK-1 Guitar Synthesizer; Tascam's Series 388 multitrack recorder; numerous synthesizers past and present from just about every manufacturer; as well as assorted pieces of equipment that I've collected over the years, from the Echoplex to the IBM PC.

I've also tried to keep all of this from being too technical. Understanding the technology used in today's music equipment is helpful, but by no means a requirement. There are dozens of other resources—including books, magazines, and video—that will explain the significance of most significant bit data for controllers with assigned numbers of 0 to 31, or will explain exponential and linear-control input of tone oscillators. So if you want to explore any of the technical details that I talk about here in greater depth, there is an abundance of material available. By the same token, I feel that you can operate a car without understanding the relationship between a combustion engine and torsion-bar suspension, or play a guitar without knowing what kind of wood glue was used in the internal bracing.

The point I'm making is that this book is designed for those of you that want to get up and do something with this technology, make it work for you, and spend as little time as possible reliving your high school science class in the process.

There are terms, phrases, and concepts that I explain because they are so often used when referring to equipment. Again, I've tried to make it as painless as possible, and have addressed it from a nontechnical standpoint. We're all musicians here; there's no need to get scary by talking about the technical ecstasy of equations for determining the composite gain of amplifiers and attenuators. As great men throughout history have been known to say, "Shut up and play your music."

It's time. Starting now, there is no turning back without everybody else passing you by. So always remember to keep moving forward, and the technology will soon be as much a part of your music as your fingers are. Ready? Set?

Go.

1

Sound

This chapter is going to tell you everything you needed to know, but never got around to asking, about the very essence of music—namely, sound. Sound is little more than the movement of air in a particular formation. Even though you don't feel it, air is pressurized around you. Without it, you would explode from the inside out, which is a pretty nasty thought. Every time you make a sound, the movement that causes that sound makes vibrations in the air pressure, which results in sound waves. When you clap your hands, yell at the top of your lungs, or strum a guitar, you are making waves in the air pressure around you. These waves are very similar to the ripples and waves that you see in water. If you're standing next to a very still pool of water and dip your finger into it, ripples emanate smoothly out from that point to all edges of the pool. Think of this as a whisper.

Now, if you drop something big into the water—like a Cadillac—then the ripples become waves that slosh all over the place and create quite a pronounced effect. Think of this water-wave movement as the sound-wave equivalent of someone screaming bloody murder, or that lady you know who has the high-pitched hysterical laugh that makes you cringe whenever she's in the room. These are major air pressure disturbances resulting in major sound waves.

In the case of sound, air is what ripples and waves, not water. Interestingly, though, if you make noise in or near water, it travels a lot more clearly and faster than it does through the air. This is because water molecules are closer together than air molecules, and thus more of them move when they are disturbed.

As the sound waves move through the air because of a vibration and the resulting air pressure, they must be picked up by a sound receiver, which in our case is the ear. Our ears (and their internal workings like eardrums, cochlea, etc.) pick up the air pressure and, in conjunction with the brain, interpret them as *sounds.* No ears around? Then there are no sounds, just air pressure. Sound waves exist only as air movements until something translates the air pressure into actual sound. If a tree falls in the woods, and nobody is around to hear it, does it make a sound? No. That's right, *no.* Sorry to break this to you, but it's true. The tree makes sound waves, but unless something is there to interpret them as sound, they just move through the air until they fade out. Of course, this doesn't count if you include birds and bears, or somebody leaving a tape deck (another sound interpreter) recording all by itself in those same woods. Those animals can hear it because they have the proper ear mechanisms, and the tape deck has manmade sensors which pick up sound waves and convert them to actual sound.

Different types of hearing devices can pick up different types of sound waves. This is why dogs can hear certain high-pitched sounds, like whistles, that we can't hear. Our sound interpretation apparatus just isn't sophisticated enough to detect those types of changes in air pressure. The same is true of recording devices. Some can detect sound that we can't, and others don't pick up all the sounds that we hear. This is usually true in the high-frequency range of sound, where a recording device or microphone may not be delicate enough to capture those high sounds, leaving us with a sense of missing brightness or clarity in a recording.

Speaking of frequency, it is one of three physical attributes of sound waves, the other two being wave shape (or wave form) and amplitude. First, frequency defines the pitch of a sound, what musicians call the "high" or "low" of a sound. Second, the wave shape represents the timbre of a sound, also called its color or tone. Finally, amplitude corresponds to how loud or soft a sound is.

An additional and very important aspect of the physical nature of sound is not physical at all. It is time. Now before we embark on a Philosophy 101 discussion of the nature of man in relation to space and time, let's look at time practically. Sound is one of the only things that man deals with which is "time-bound," meaning time is an inextricable part of sound. You can't freeze an actual sound at a particular point in time and expect to be able to recognize that sound. You always have to view sound as a segment of time. For example, we can take a picture of an event and freeze it in time with a photograph, without regard to time. The photograph captures the specific essence of that event without any difficulty. More specifically, think of the movies. A film is actually a series of still photographs run in quick succession (24 frames per second), one after another. Each still captures an exact moment in time.

Try doing this with a sound—*any* sound. You cannot point to a frozen moment of time as you can with a photograph and say, "Oh, there's that sound." A sound has to be re-created at another point in time to be captured, and that re-creation involves making or playing that sound over a few seconds or minutes or hours of *time*. I hope all of this makes sense, because it tends to be fairly obvious. If it isn't, one method of proving this is to find a defective compact disk or CD player. On a defective disk, a segment of music only a fraction of a second long tends to loop itself continuously and very quickly. The resulting piece of music does not capture any of the essence of the song and is usually unrecognizable as a part of a particular song. This is because it requires a period of time longer than a fraction of a second for you to even recognize the resulting noise as music in the first place.

Do the same thing with a tape deck. Clip a length of tape about 1/8th of an inch long and splice it onto a blank segment of tape. When playing it through the tape deck, see if you get anything other than a quick "bleep" of sound that doesn't make much sense. Even though this is a primitive example, it's almost like taking a snapshot of the sound or music. Yet you're still playing that sound through time, whether it's one second or 1/100th of a second; you're still using time to get even a snapshot level of sound. You see the difficulty in extricating sound from time? It's impossible.

We can, however, look at representations of what a moment of sound looks like. These representations are positioned along a normal X and Y axis diagram like you might have used in grade school to measure the growth of populations per year, or how tall you grew every year. The X axis represented years (time) and the Y axis represented amounts of growth or population at each point in time—literally, the *what* that happens over time.

Here are some quick examples. In Figure 1–1, the difference between the two pictures is the number of waves created over time, or the frequency. Note that these are examples of tones which do not change over time. Although such kinds of frequencies can be generated with electronic

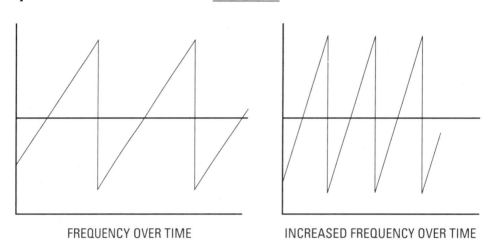

FREQUENCY OVER TIME   INCREASED FREQUENCY OVER TIME

Figure 1-1.   Variation in frequency (pitch) of a sound wave.

equipment, natural sounds all fade (decay) or change over time (an in-depth discussion of this occurs in Chapter Five).

In Figure 1–2, the difference is the timbre, or actual shape of the waveform over time.

The only difference in the two pictures in Figure 1–3 is the amplitude, or how loud the sound is.

Finally, the two diagrams in Figure 1–4 differ in every respect; there is no sameness in frequency, wave shape, or amplitude between the two.

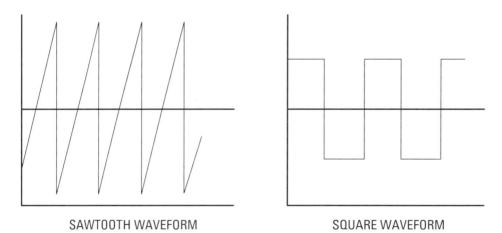

SAWTOOTH WAVEFORM   SQUARE WAVEFORM

Figure 1-2.   Variation in shape (timbre) of a sound wave.

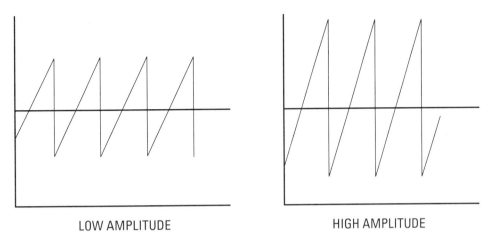

LOW AMPLITUDE   HIGH AMPLITUDE

Figure 1–3.   Variation in amplitude (volume) of a sound wave.

How do we get these nifty diagrams? They are really graphic representations of sound taken as electrical response to the air pressure of sound waves. When a microphone or pickup is hit with sound waves, either a diaphragm (in the case of the microphone) or a sensitive magnetic field (in the case of the pickup) is vibrated, much like the pool of water described earlier. Only instead of water ripples, these mechanisms send electrical impulses in response to the waves. The impulses are sent to an amplifier which in turn strengthens these pulses and sends them to

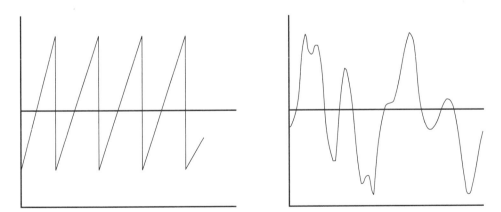

Figure 1–4.   Variations in all properties (frequency, shape, and amplitude) of two sound waves.

a speaker. The speaker then vibrates in sympathy with the strong electrical signal it receives and pushes that sound *back* into the air. Then—ta da—your ear picks up these speaker waves as sound. A good way to examine this is to take the front screen away from a stereo speaker, and watch how sound (especially very strong and very low bass notes, like a kick drum) will force air out of the speakers and create very noticeable air pressure.

All of this can be observed with an oscilloscope—a device that creates visual representations of waveforms, like those shown in Figure 1–4.

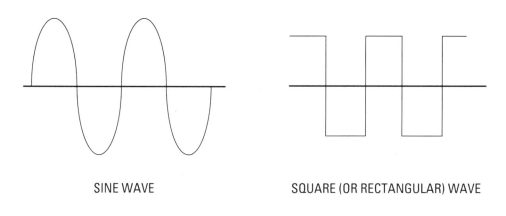

SINE WAVE   SQUARE (OR RECTANGULAR) WAVE

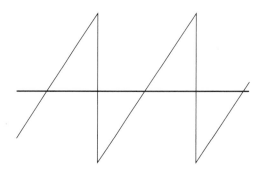

SAWTOOTH WAVE

Figure 1–5. Variations in waveform.

And the properties of sound represented on the X and Y graph can be described with very scientific-sounding terms. For instance:

- *Hertz* is a measure of frequency, one Hertz being equal to one complete cycle per second. It is called Hertz simply because it is named for the man who defined the measurement, H. R. Hertz. It's abbreviated as Hz. The lower the Hertz, the lower the frequency, the deeper the tone. Low Hz levels produce bass tones, high Hz levels produce treble tones.

- Amplitude is discussed in terms of *decibels* (dBs), or loudness units. Unfortunately, the measurement of exactly what constitutes a decibel is based on a bizarre algorithm that even most physics professors have a hard time understanding. Suffice it to say that normal conversation occurs at about 60 dBs, planes taking off create a roar of about 120 dBs, and your eardrums are in serious danger of meltdown around 160 dBs.

- Waveforms are usually defined by their shapes, or obvious and regularly occurring characteristics. Those shapes are sine waves, square waves, and sawtooth waves (Fig. 1–5).

Those are really the basics of sound. Although you didn't expect to get a crash course in the physics of wave formation and movement, don't you feel better about everything now that you've learned all this neat stuff? Everything you read from here on, though, is devoted to the whys, whats, and hows of making sound into music with modern equipment. And no more physics lessons.

2

The History of Electronic Music Technology

lectricity is still a mystery to most people. Despite its pervasiveness in our culture and in our every waking moment, few of us understand what electricity is or does. Sure, it powers our TVs and microwaves, and keeps the lights going when it gets dark. But how and why this happens is still something that eludes even the most curious of minds.

In a time before electricity, things were easier to understand. In order to create light, you touched a piece of ignited wood to a strip of cloth dipped in oil, and the oil burned, making a flame, creating light. The same was true for the stove or driving steam engines. Back then, you could see what course of events led to the creation of light, heat, power.

Music was the same way not so long ago. You plucked on a string and it vibrated, creating sound. You blew air through a horn, and depending on the certain way the horn curved and flared, a certain sound came out. You pounded on a keyboard and hammers hit varying widths and lengths of strings, creating various sounds. You opened your mouth, and songs came out.

The active process of creating music was once as *visible* a medium as it was an *audible* medium. Before the recording processes of the late 1800s and the early 1900s were introduced, all music was performed live; you could *see* the music being made. Fingers plucked, bows stroked, mallets hit, horns blared; music was *made*.

Making Electricity into Music

The introduction of electricity into the making of music has created a class of instruments and recording processes which are as alien to our basic understanding of musical creation as the workings of a microwave. We still use these new electronic instruments—in fact, they are now accounting for most of the music we encounter—we just don't understand them in the way we used to understand our more basic acoustic, *visible* music instruments.

All of which is too bad, because much as the creation of the radio, television, VCR, and microwave have enhanced our enjoyment of certain pastimes, as well as given us an appreciation of technology, the implementation of electronic music technology can be similarly valuable. The intricacies of today's musical instruments tend to scare users, but a quick learning curve can easily surmount those fears. For instance, today's compact disk player is to yesterday's crank-up Victrola record player as today's synthesizers are to yesterday's harpsichords. Can you imagine the residents of Mayberry, North Carolina, having to confront a push-button phone with call forwarding, call waiting, two incoming lines, and a hold button? No way. It was only two decades ago that some places still relied on crank phones and a local operator to make calls. And the leap in technologies hasn't been all that great conceptually, it has just followed a natural progression, like the wood stove to the microwave.

As an aside, it is essential to recognize the importance of one machine in the overall scheme of electronic music technology: the phonograph. Though not an electrical invention, Thomas Alva Edison's first phonograph player, created in 1877, heralded the era of recorded music. Edison's tin-foil tube and needle device, while far removed from anything even remotely resembling today's record players, allowed music to be captured in a very literal sense. No longer did music have to be a function of live performance; it could now be "stored" for use whenever one desired to hear it. The barriers between live and recorded music were shattered forever. Ultimately, the application of electricity in the early 1900s to this device, as well as to sound-creation instruments, changed the scope of music permanently.

The first attempts at breaking music and sound creation away from traditional instruments were begun shortly after the turn of this century. In 1906, the Telharmonium was demonstrated in the United States by its inventor, Thaddeus Cahill. The 200-ton machine (roughly the weight of 125 Rolls Royces, or more appropriately, 400 grand pianos) consisted of a rotating cam which was able to generate notes of the Western tonal scale, yet the machine contained no "modern" electronic devices such as vacuum tubes or amplifiers. This instrument was the predecessor of the modern electric organ more than it was a forerunner of synthesizers. Interestingly, *The Random House Dictionary* defines a telharmonium as "a musical keyboard instrument operating by alternating currents of electricity which, on impulse from the keyboard, produce music at a distant point via phone lines." Precursor to modern MIDI systems, perhaps?

Some 20 years later, two Frenchmen—Eduoard Coupleux and Joseph Givelet—invented the first electronic synthesizer. Though the machine was called an "automatically operating musical instrument of the electric oscillation type," and *not* a synthesizer, it contained all the rudiments and principles of what synthesizers were to become. By expanding on the then-popular format of the player piano—which uses holes punched in paper tape to trigger or indicate certain notes—the two inventors made provisions for more holes which would have control over tone, pitch, and loudness of sound. For those not familiar with the workings of a player piano, a roll of paper with holes punched in it, much like fabled IBM cards, moves past a sounding board within the piano, sounding keys that correspond to the holes in the paper. A similar operation is found in a simple music box, which uses a metallic roller with protrusions to "pick" metal tuning bars.

Coupleux and Givelet took the paper roll one step further and gave it more control over the machine. Whereas player pianos couldn't, and still can't, affect the coloration of a note, the Frenchmen added holes to their paper to control other parts of the machine, namely oscillators and filters. By activating a certain combination of these elements at a specific time, effects such as tremolo could be added to the note and actually controlled. The instrument demonstrated that a non-acoustic instrument could generate the same breadth of expression as an acoustic instrument, offering gradations of tone color along with pitch variation. It's important to note that tones are easily generated by electricity; you hear them from power plants, you hear them in loose wiring, you hear them in generators. However, tones do not constitute music. It is the control of tones and the addition of expression (what musicians call brightness and color) that make such tones recognizable as music. The Coupleux-Givelet machine was the first to offer such electrical control.

A number of advances were made after World War I in the "synthesizing" or artificial creation of sounds, primarily in France, Russia, and Germany. Leon Theremin created an instrument in 1920 called the aetherophone, which is better known by its inventor's last name, the theremin. This device sent a signal generated by a vacuum tube up a single antenna-like spire, and then was "played" by the performer who placed his or her left and right hand at different positions in relation to the antenna, thus generating different frequencies and amplification. The sound was popularized by the Beach Boys, who used the theremin for the weird effect on "Good Vibrations," and Led Zeppelin's Jimmy Page, who employed the instrument in concert performances of the group's "Whole Lotta Love."

Another "synthesizer," the Trautonium, was created in 1930 by Friedrich Trautwein. A monophonic machine, the Trautonium used a neon tube as its oscillator, and utilized a wire stretched across a metal bar for pitch changes. Anytime the performer pressed the foot pedal which was connected to the wire, the wire touched the metal bar and completed a circuit, emitting a specific sound. A two-voice version of the Trautonium showed up a few years later as the Mixtur-Trautonium.

More variations of the electronic organ continued to appear in a variety of incarnations during this period. Jorg Mager's Spaerophone, Richard Ranger's Rangertone, Bruno Helberger and Peter Lertes' Hellertion, and the Partiturophone were all part of a considerable international movement to create a truly *electronic* instrument. Yet these instruments came and went, as others improved upon the concept of an electricity-driven organ. Laurens Hammond's development of the fully-integrated electric organ in 1934 made most of these instruments obsolete. The legendary Hammond organ, immortalized in everything from church choirs to daytime game shows, remains the standard by which all other electronic organs are measured. (See Fig. 2–1.)

But the electric organ was merely a modern-day equivalent of something which already existed. The effort to create new, different, and unusual sounds for musical use was pursued relentlessly. The breakthrough in this pursuit was the founding of Pierre Schaeffer and Pierre Henry's

Figure 2-1.   Hammond organ.

Radiodiffusion studio in Paris in 1948. The purpose of this studio was the creation and performance of *musique concrète,* the use of natural sounds to create music. Schaeffer set up a studio in which recorded sounds of natural events—singing birds, rustling leaves, babbling brooks, snarling traffic— could be pieced together in different ways to make music. This was done by arranging the sequence of sounds on a *phonograph* record. For the first time, composers were exposed to the notion that musical compositions did not have to be created on traditional musical instruments; indeed, compos- ers didn't even require instruments of any sort, only the ability to manipu- late sounds.

At the same time, Radio Cologne in Germany was set up as a studio very similar to the Radiodiffusion of Paris. However, the studio, directed by Friedrich Enke, opted to use new "electronic" instruments for music creation instead of pursue the *musique concrète* method of using recorded sounds. In 1952, the station asked Friedrich Trautwein—of Trautonium fame—to develop an instrument for use in creating electronic sound. The resulting instrument was the Monochord, an electronic extension of the earlier Trautonium. It gave way soon thereafter to Harold Bode's Melochord, which was a polyphonic electronic version of the Mixtur-Trautonium that used two keyboards. With these instruments, using pure electronically generated sounds for music became a tangible part of composing "modern music," and a number of European composers began to include electrically generated music in their musical scores.

THE ADVENT OF COMPUTERS

At this point, the worlds of computers and music start to collide. In the 1940s, spurred on by World War II, the United States started using computers for processing war data—everything from weather to troop movements. These roomsized contraptions, beginning with ENIAC (Electronic Numeric Integrator And Calculator) in 1945, bear almost no resemblance to the computers we use today. In fact, most of the original computers had less memory than a credit-card-sized calculator. Activated by throwing switches, using up to 18,000 vacuum tubes, drawing 250 kilowatts of electricity, and storing memory in large cells, these computers were nonetheless in the forefront of technology at the time. As they improved, so did the methods of making them operate, or programming them. No visual monitors or typewriter keyboards were used for input, however. Computers were programmed by inserting paper tape punched with holes to code routines into the machine. Paper tape also served as the memory storage for large amounts of information. Yes, paper tape, the kind that was originally found on player pianos and Coupleux-Givelets' early electric oscillator. The same kind of paper tape is still used in sending telex messages, and in a slightly modified form as IBM cards, which seem to be present only in government agencies and in university registration offices. Right up to the 1970s, paper tape and paper IBM cards were the preferred means of electronic information storage. Floppy disks and RAM were twinkles in almost nobody's eyes.

In 1955, Radio Corporation of America (RCA) introduced the first "synthesizer," developed by Herbert Belar and Harry Olsen. Built for the purpose of studying the nature of sound, the machine operated using paper tape to control changes in its oscillators. But RCA, which was involved in much of the recording work going on in the 1950s, saw no reason to manufacture more than a few prototypes of this machine—the first commercial one was called the Mark II (Fig. 2–2). One of the reasons for discontinuing the synthesizer was the difficulty in controlling the information on paper tapes. They were not readable to the human eye, and out-of-place holes also produced wrong sounds. Its sheer size and cost were another factor.

The Mark II was not a synthesizer that we think of in the current sense, in terms of size and appearance. Based loosely on the ENIAC computer design, the original RCA Mark synthesizer that was developed in the late 1940s was a room-sized behemoth. It wasn't scaled down much by the mid-1950s, either. The Mark II was set up at Columbia University, where a great deal of academic electronic musical research was carried out at the time. Something better and more workable had to be developed for the creative musician.

Figure 2-2.   **RCA Mark II at RCA Laboratories, Princeton, N.J.**

Something was; Robert Moog, a doctoral student at Cornell University, invented the voltage-controlled oscillator. This allowed oscillator tone to be shaped and colored by modifying the voltage applied. Moog built this oscillator, along with an amplifier, into a module that could be controlled in much the same way as telephone operating systems were controlled, using patch bays. Using cables to patch together different sections of the module, Moog's invention could be programmed in almost real-time. An adept and adroit musician could plug cables into arrangements that offered new sounds, new tones, new effects in the same way that telephone operators could route new calls from place to place simply by making the connection with a cable. At the same time, Donald Buchla invented a similar machine, but its means of input was a touch-sensitive metal plate that replaced the keyboard. Although this machine was embraced by entities such as Columbia University, Buchla's use of plates instead of movable keys has placed him in a position second to Moog's in the annals of early synthesizer development.

FROM ANALOG TO DIGITAL SYNTHESIS

Moog's first synthesizer, a series of connected modules and oscillators introduced to the public at a 1964 trade show—and many of the other similar advancements made in early synthesis by people including Max Mathews of Bell Labs, Donald Buchla, and Alan R. Pearlman—ushered in the age of electronic analog musical synthesizers. For the next two decades, commercial synthesizer development would follow along the lines set by these developers. An intrinsic part—as well as a limitation—of this development was the fact that these machines were all *analog* devices.

All of these synthesizers were created to take advantage of electrical current flowing through various parts of the synth, from oscillators, to filters, to amplifiers. Hence the term *analog*. The concept of something being an analog device has to do with the physical movement of that device. For example, watches with hour, minute, and sweep second hands are analog devices. On the other hand, a watch that simply displays the numeric representation of time is a digital device. The analog device shows time through physical movement, the digital device performs the same function by displaying the representation of time as determined by binary code—the 1s and 0s that make up today's digital computer languages. The same is true for a car that shows miles per hour with a meter. That is analog. A current-model luxury car shows increase in speed by displaying the speed not by gradually moving a pointer upward, but by increasing the value of numbers in a digital display.

One critical aspect of music technology, that of recording, has until very recently been a completely analog business. But digital recording is taking over the process of recording music, and understanding the difference between analog and digital will become very important as the following chapters unfold. The process of cutting grooves into wax and vinyl is perhaps the most obvious form of analog, or physical, recording. The manipulation of magnetic ferrites on a strip of tape by pulsing electric signals across it is as much an analog format as is the cutting of records. Taking these pulses or signals and converting them into a digital form (1s and 0s) is rapidly creating a type of recorded sound almost indistinguishable from a live performance, and as such, digital recording is becoming pervasive throughout the music industry.

Back to synthesizers. Control over electronically-generated tones, packaged in a usable form based on Moog's initial precepts, made the synthesizer an incredibly popular instrument in the 1970s. Moog himself introduced the next step in synthesizer technology by replacing much of the patching of cords and cables with easier-to-manipulate knobs and dials. Now synthesizers began to look more like their computer counterparts and less like the local telephone switching station. (See Fig. 2–3.) However, the problem still remained, as it did in the computer industry, of having to fine-tune and adjust the output of the synthesizers by hand. Whereas dials and switches had replaced paper tape and a Medusa's head of patch cables, the dials still had to be tweaked and switches thrown anytime a modification to the system was needed. In effect, the synthesizer's biggest problem was that it had no memory. Rick Wakeman, former keyboard player of the progressive rock group Yes, has pointed out that in the early days (mid-1970s) he might spend half an hour setting up the proper positions on his live set-up of synthesizer keyboards to obtain a sound that would last for only 30 seconds during a concert. Hence, these synths were suitable for people with either a great deal of patience or a great ability to remember individual patch positions for individual sounds. Going from a simulated jet engine sound to one that sounded like sweeping symphonic strings might require reconfiguring the entire setup from scratch.

Figure 2-3.   Moog synthesizer.

All of this twiddling and tweaking was necessary because of the synthesizer's analog roots. Since the flow of electricity was actually being modified *physically* by changing dial settings or rearranging patch cords, physical adjustments were required. One couldn't store a live electronic charge in memory components for use at some later date. That would be like trying to record a TV program for future viewing by trying to trap the actual transmitted signal. The answer came in the form of the microprocessor. The microprocessor is at the heart of all computers and calculators that we use today. If the truth be known, they also control an incredible number of the functions of automobiles, microwaves, VCRs, and time-activated coffeemakers. Microprocessors can take the power and the mechanisms inherent in all those little switches, dials, vacuum tubes, and what-not, and shrink them down to the size of a child's fingernail. The functions carried out by those 18,000 vacuum tubes in the ENIAC can now be performed comfortably by a chip of silicon that you can barely see.

With the advent of microprocessors, true "computer control" in an efficient and economical form came to synthesizers. The first commercial use came in the form of the Prophet-5, a programmable synthesizer from an American company known as Sequential Circuits (the same company that proposed the MIDI specification for music data exchange). The company took the concept of patch cabling and knob twisting and created a synthesizer that stored the combinations and dial settings in microprocessor memory so that they could be retrieved with the touch of a single button. If a user wanted to recall certain sound configurations, he or she could set up the machine to produce the desired sound, and then store that configuration to memory. This worked in much the same way as memory-dial phones remember telephone numbers after they've been punched into a memory.

With this kind of control, analog synths reached what would become their final frontier—final, because of an inherent condition of analog technology. The problem of trying to emulate real sounds, such as a true cello or a true vocal choir, was almost insurmountable with analog technology because of the number of variables that go into creating, say, a true violin sound—reverberation, pitch, tone, brightness, attack, delay, release, sustain, decay, air, ambient noise, construction materials such as wood and resins, and on and on. Since the synthesizer generated all of its sounds electronically, there was often a lack of natural depth and resonance, as well as peripheral, unwanted electrical noise and undertones. By the early 1980s, though, programmable analog synthesizers had found a niche in generating the weird, unusual, and fascinating sounds that went into the then-popular music craze of techno-pop, sounds employed by such artists as Thomas Dolby, Howard Jones, and later, the Pet Shop Boys. Synthesizer sounds were being used as true and natural sounds in their own right, without much intent to "synthesize" natural acoustic sounds. With the demise of techno-pop, in 1984–1985, concern in the electronic music community returned to the creation of synthesizer sounds that sounded more like other instruments.

Having reached its analog summit, the breakthrough in achieving ultimate control over the synthesizer came through the use of one medium—digital technology.

Digital technology is what drives all of today's computers. Instead of the manipulation of electric currents and the physical rearrangement of electricity found in analog devices, digital technology cleans it all up by breaking it into binary code. This means that every electronic pulse, signal, message, and motion is represented as a combination of 1s and 0s. The arrangement of these two digits provides for a much more specific representation of a given event than analog. That, for instance, is why wearers of digital watches will give you the exact time—it's 11:02:53— and why wearers of analog watches will usually say it's a little past 11, or it's almost five after 11. Digital representation is an exact representation, because it freezes a moment or an event in time and assigns it a value. Similarly, it eliminates moving pieces, much like a hand-held calculator replaces the movements of the analog-based abacus. Less moving parts, less breakdown to worry about.

Synthesizer developers realized that with digital representation they could *exactly* simulate a sound event. By assigning a digital value to all of the idiosyncrasies of a sound wave, a much more accurate "natural" sound could be achieved instead of trying to do it by adjusting values manually in an analog synth.

BRINGING DIGITAL SYNTHESIS OUT OF THE LABS

As much as digital synthesis represented a breakthrough for synthesizer development, the commercial availability was a little trickier. With a price tag equivalent to four or five Ferraris (base price of $250,000), New England Digital introduced the Synclavier synthesizer to the professional market in 1980. The synthesizer was actually as much a computer as it was a synthesizer, but it did represent an astounding application of digital technology. Clearly, though, the Synclavier and its similarly-priced Australian competitor, the Fairlight, were not models of price/performance efficiency. It was only a matter of time before the consumer- and mass-market-oriented synth makers who had been serving their customers with analog machines got into the digital race. More importantly, in looking for economical ways of employing digital technology, these companies developed and implemented new processes for developing digital sound.

One of the first off the mark was the maker of the pervasive plastic digital watches, Casio. Using a technology known as phase distortion and based on its proprietary CZ algorithm, the company introduced the CZ-101 digital synthesizer in 1983 at just under $500. At the same time, Yamaha introduced its DX Series digital synthesizers, based on frequency modulation (FM) synthesis. This technology was developed during the 1970s by

Stanford University researcher John Chowning at the Center for Computer Research into Music and Acoustics. Yamaha licensed the technology from Stanford and proceeded to manufacture what is currently the all-time best-selling synth in the world, the DX-7. Although this model has been supplanted by more enhanced DX versions, and supplemented by other models (Fig. 2–4), it is still considered to be the pivotal instrument which spread digital synthesis to the consumer market.

Not to be outdone, other manufacturers have introduced new variations on digital technology. Roland introduced the D-50 synthesizer in 1986, a machine based on linear arithmetic synthesis. Kurzweil Music Systems has its Kurzweil 250, which actually employs algorithms generated by artificial intelligence techniques to create genuinely acoustic sounds. These machines use custom-designed microprocessors known as Very Large Scale Integrated (VSLI) processors, which provide the synthesizers with even more capability, memory, and functions. It allows for onboard sequencing (digital recording), storing of sound and patch changes, layering sounds on top of each other over different parts of the keyboard, or assigning individual sounds to individual keys. It becomes obvious very quickly how digital technology and microprocessor circuitry have brought us quite some distance from the telephone-operator designs of the first synths.

An interesting drawback to the use of digital synths is that their success in creating natural sounds has been *so* close to complete that these

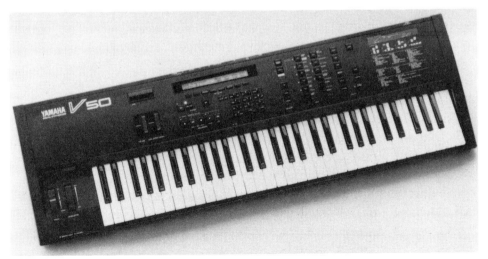

Figure 2–4. Yamaha V50 digital synthesizer.

synths can't create the original kinds of sounds generated by the early Moog and ARP analog synthesizers. The sizzling electronic stabs and truncated sound patterns that could be created have almost disappeared from the new generation of synths because of their exactness and accuracy. Unless one has a strange sound installed in the memory of the digital synth that can be modified, no "synthesizer" sounds can be created. This, again, is due to the fact that analog synthesis created sounds by adding or subtracting from an electronic signal. In digital synthesis, the sound and its structure already exists, to be modified only slightly by the user. The parameters of a digitally represented sound can't just be "shoved around" or "knocked about" like analog sounds with the pushing of switches and turning of dials. Digital sounds adhere to a fixed numerical representation which holds as tightly as a pit bull's jaws. Reprogramming a digital sound is not done on the fly, as analog programming was done; indeed, sometimes reprogramming digital sounds on a synthesizer closely resembles programming a computer application.

Finally, digital technology in synthesizers has taken us to what may be the summit of synthesizer technology: sampling. Sampling allows a digitally recorded sound—which could be anything from breaking glass to a human voice to an oboe (à la *musique concrète*)—to be played as if it were an instrument. Hence, a voice recorded as saying "Good morning, how are you?" could be entered into the sampling synthesizer's memory and storage medium, and then accessed as a regular part of the sound arsenal. Pressing the A key below middle C on the keyboard would generate the words "Good morning, how are you?" in the pitch of A. The same is true with the F# key two octaves above middle C, or any other key on the keyboard. This means that because of digital sampling, every sound known to man could theoretically be played on a synthesizer. With the addition of MIDI, which will be discussed later, a synthesizer that doesn't have sampling capabilities can even access one that does.

Digital recording is also replacing our traditional concepts of using tape for recording material. By digitizing all inputs (vocals, instruments, percussion, effects, etc.) and dropping them right onto a magnetic disk, a new level of control over the work is achieved. Events can be examined in real-time, without having to rewind or fast-forward. Instruments and voices can be speeded up without altering the pitch, a huge advantage over tape. While this process is still very expensive, it reproduces sound with a clarity almost indistinguishable from the original sound source.

BETTER MUSIC THROUGH ELECTRONIC TECHNOLOGY

Looking at the history of *electronic* music technology is different from examining other technologies applied to music, such as the improved resins and glues that make brighter-sounding violin bodies, or the fiberglass molding that strengthens the construction of a guitar. Electronic technology is singular in its evolution, rapid as that evolution may have been to get us to where we are today. Though the history of applied electronic music technology is relatively short in length, it contains much more information than can be covered in any single chapter or perhaps any single readable volume.

Unlike other forms of musical expression which date back to times primeval, electronic music technology is very traceable—we know where to find the source of individual developments, from Thomas Edison's use of electricity for sound re-creation to Pierre Schaeffer's *musique concrète* to Robert Moog's first synth to John Chowning's FM research. Between these historical landmarks lie hundreds of other important achievements in combining music with modern advancements in technology, as well as hundreds of other people. On the pages that follow, you will have a chance to see what these achievements and people have wrought in the pursuit of innovative music technology.

3

Computers

erhaps the most intimidating aspect of dealing with technology is working with computers. Ever since science fiction stories and movies depicted computers as runaway machines bent on destroying their human masters in such thrillers as *2001: A Space Odyssey, The Forbin Project,* or *War Games,* most people get unnerved about sitting in front of these ominous electrical creatures. But like cars, guitars, and toasters, computers don't do anything without humans directing them. Computers are not alive, and cannot think in any way, shape, or form. They can, however, calculate the difference between a 1 and a 0 faster than you can blink, which is about all that they have to do. We shall soon see that this seeming limitation produces phenomenal results.

Basically, computers only understand the process of adding 1 and 0, which I will describe fully in a minute. They have no understanding of value, or what anything means, and they have no intrinsic intelligence. When adding these 1s and 0s, they produce calculations which have been given some meaning by human programmers. Thus, adding eight 1s to eight 0s may give us a calculation that some programmer has determined should equal the word "the." The computer doesn't know what "the" means, it only knows to add up the proper number of 1s and 0s to produce "the" on your screen. It's like a dog retrieving a newspaper. The dog knows you want the newspaper, but it doesn't know that you are going to read it, or that you are checking the comics to get your daily grins. The dog has no concept of "reading," or of what the paper's value is, but it does know how to get the paper and bring it to you.

Computer fear arises from the feeling that computers can do serious damage to things like your tax return or credit rating, which they can. However, computers have no more intelligence than guns or cars. That may seem unusual, but it is quite true, since they are simply machines. I will not try to convince you that computers are perfectly harmless because they are brainless machines. Brainless machines also shoot people and run over them on dark deserted streets. As with any machine, the control is in the hands of the user, and computers are no exception. They work well when someone who understands them—and isn't afraid to make a few mistakes along the way—makes the effort to use them efficiently.

Regardless of your direct experience with personal computers or the mainframes that keep records for everybody from the IRS to the CIA, you have probably had some experience with computing in your home. Can you program your VCR to record a movie while you're not home? Can you set your microwave to melt your cheese sandwich instead of nuking it into atomic oblivion? Then you can program computers. The devices I've just described use the same electronic "brains" that computers use. These brains are actually little slivers of silicon called microprocessors. These microprocessors go by esoteric names such as the Motorola 68030 or the Intel 80386 or the Zilog Z-80. IBM computers use the Intel microprocessors while Apples use the Motorola variety, just as a Toyota uses a four-cylinder engine and a Cadillac uses a six- or eight-cylinder engine. These are simply different methods from different manufacturers for powering the machine.

Microprocessors are also called chips, because they are actually small pieces or chips of large silicon wafers. Silicon wafers are purified sheets of sand that are excellent for conducting and controlling a particular flow of electricity. These chips have microscopic etchings and layers of channels and paths which determine the flow of electricity through them.

Look at the inside of a distortion pedal or chorus device, or even the inside of a telephone. All of the little transistors, wires, and resistors that you see on the small plastic board can be shrunken down to microscopic size on a given chip. Actually, some chips have dozens of different kinds of functions compacted onto one chip, which usually results in a microcomputer or, as it is most commonly known, a personal computer (PC).

The next few paragraphs will offer a basic introduction to PCs. Much of the technology discussed here is also discussed in Chapter Four, since MIDI is based on the use of microprocessors. For those who are already familiar with the technology, this section will be a quick review. For those who have no clue whatsoever as to what goes on inside a personal computer, sit back for the next few minutes, take a deep breath (but don't hold it), and plunge in.

How Computers Work

Computers consist of two primary elements: a processor and some memory. A processor handles electrical signals, and a memory stores information. Think of it in terms of the human brain. While your eyes are reading a book (inputting information), your brain is sorting through the words and making sense of them (processing the information), and then putting it somewhere deep inside your memory for future reference (data storage and memory). You may read *Gone with the Wind* and not remember a single word, but that is because your memory is so vast that you have difficulty recalling particular passages in the book. Plus—and this is the most likely scenario—you probably didn't care too much about what was in the book anyway, and your memory buried it as deep as it could go, probably in there with other important stuff like your third-grade report card and what you had for breakfast a month ago Tuesday. A computer, however, remembers every piece of data that it receives until it is deleted or erased. This is why computers are excellent for storing information about bank accounts, inventories, or even names and addresses of lots of people.

Like the brain, a processor and memory are necessary for a computer's operation. Everything else is also necessary, but not as vital as these two elements. For instance, an input device can be a typewriter keyboard, a joystick, or that funny little rolling pointer called a mouse. Output can be on your screen or a written printout.

The memory stores information, and the processor allows you to get to that information, alter it, and put new information back into the memory. The microprocessor (so called because of its microscopic nature) directs the commands that you put in from a typewriter keyboard or a joystick or any other manner of input, including a music keyboard. You get a response to the information from a written printout, a monitor screen, or from a sound source such as a sound module or synth. That's all there is to it. A computer simply processes and stores information.

Here's how it all works: Electricity pulses through the system in bursts equivalent to 1 and 0. Each burst of 1 means "ON," each burst equaling 0 means "OFF." Since electricity moves at the speed of light, the activity here sends through ON and OFF messages at an extremely high rate of speed, such that billions of these messages are pulsed through the processor every second. At such a rate, information is being pulsed through in nano- and picoseconds—one-billionth and one-trillionth of a second, respectively— something you could never measure, watch, or hope to keep up with. As a matter of fact, the transistors on a microprocessor can switch between 1 and 0 at a rate of 750 picoseconds. Try dividing one second by one trillion. Try dividing a second by even ten or two. If you're like most people, you can't even begin to comprehend anything happening this fast. We are talk- ing serious speed here.

With two different kinds of electrical bursts, ON and OFF, the most practical method of creating information from these bursts is to use calcu- lations that are always based on 2 (ON/OFF, IN/OUT, YES/NO). Fortu- nately, a type of mathematics based on arrangements of two components has existed for a very long time, and is called binary math. Our standard math is based primarily on the decimal system and the numbers 0 through 9, which is ten digits in all. Zero is extremely important here, because it allows us to create multiples of all the other numbers by allowing for a blank space (20, 30, 40, etc.) that doesn't have to be filled with something from 1 through 9. Very important, that zero. The early Egyptians who created the Pyramids and the Sphinx had no concept of zero, and it screwed them up for centuries. So zero is a big deal.

Even though we use the decimal system based on ten digits as our primary method for calculating everything from pocket change to how old we are, other forms of math are useful for more intricate calculations, especially those used in science and engineering. We use decimal math by simply adding a "tens" place (represented by 0) to a "ones" place (1 through 9). Another 0 gives us a "hundreds" place, two more than that gives us a "thousands" place, and so on. I know this sounds like a third-grade arith- metic class, but bear with me.

Now, binary math only has two components—0 and 1—and all infor- mation and all values are computed with just these two numbers. Binary calculations have the same ultimate value as decimal calculations, but their manner of representation is different. Say you have the number 79. In our normal method of performing mathematical calculations, we've learned that this is equal to seven sets of 10 (7×10) and nine sets of 1 (9×1). Together these two sets total up to 79. Easy enough.

With binary numbers, everything is a multiple of 2. Instead of the decimal system where you have columns for tens, hundreds, and thousands, you now have twos, fours, eights, sixteens, thirty-twos, and so on. In decimal terms, we arrive at our different "place" levels by multiplying ten by itself over and over. 10×10 is 100, $\times 10$ more is 1000, $\times 10$ more is 10,000, $\times 10$ more is 100,000, $\times 10$ more is 1,000,000. Binary goes through this same process with twos. 2×2 is 4, $\times 2$ more is 8, $\times 2$ more is 16, $\times 2$ more is 32, $\times 2$ more is 64, $\times 2$ more is 128, on into infinity.

Keeping this in mind—and I promise you'll *never* have to do another binary calculation after this—we can represent 79 in binary by expanding it out to the various twos columns. Since we only have 0 and 1, only 0 and 1 can go in each column. 1 means that we activate that column—a 1 in column 64 means the value of that column is 64—and 0 means that we skip it. We have columns headed 1, 2, 4, 8, 16, 32, 64, and 128. Now let's do a little simple calculating. 79 is smaller than 128, so we can't put a 1 in that column, so it gets a 0. However, the next column is 64, which is less than 79. 64 goes into 79 once, so we put a 1 in the 64 column, with 15 left over. Now we've got to figure out how to arrive at the remaining 15 digits. Moving over to the 32 column, we find it's bigger than 15, and so it gets a 0, as does the 16 column. The 8 column works, though, so we put a 1 in it, which gives us a 1 in both the 64 and 8 columns, for a total of 72. The remaining 7 are a piece of cake. The 4 column gets a 1 (giving us 76), the 2 column gets a 1 (making it 78), and then the 1 column gets a 1, which gives us the total of 79. What we have ends up looking like this:

$$(0 \times 128) + (1 \times 64) + (0 \times 32) + (0 \times 16) + (1 \times 8) + (1 \times 4) + (1 \times 2) + (1 \times 1)$$

Putting together the 1s and 0s in order, this binary number is 01001111, which gives us the same value as the decimal 79. All eight columns are necessary to make up a complete piece of information that can be understood by a computer.

Okay, end of math lesson. Suffice it to say that the two components in binary math are as powerful as our normal calculations using ten, even though it may take longer. However, this makes it perfect for computers, which use electrical pulses at such a high speed, the extra time is never noticed. Plus, all the computer has to do is add up all the information as a series of ON/OFFs, or 1/0s.

Each one of these 0s and 1s is called a binary digit, or bit. Get it? (*B*inary dig*IT*) A group of eight *bits* is called a *byte.* In the computer world, one byte is the smallest piece of complete information you can use. In binary code, the eight bits of a byte can give us numerical values of zero through 255, or 256 in total. If you've ever played around with computer memory or storage, this number should sound familiar to you. When we went through the twos column in the last paragraph, we went in multiples of two up the scale: 2, 4, 8, 16, 32, 64, and 128. The next logical number would be 256, since it is 2×128. When people discuss memory in a PC they always talk about "256 kilobytes" or "512 kilobytes" of memory. These numbers always seem odd until you realize that they are simply extensions of the binary series. Hence the reason for machines like the Commodore 64 or the Macintosh 512.

We've seen that an eight-bit byte can give us 256 different configurations. If we extend the size of that byte to 16 bits (8×2), we can now get 65,536 different binary variations (ranging from 16 1s to 16 0s). And the multiple goes up if we stretch our bytes out to 32 bits or 64 bits. The current state of PCs, though, only lets the microprocessors handle either 16 or 32 bits, and 64 bits won't become common practice until well into the 1990s. Twenty years ago, the fastest computers only handled four-bit bytes.

These electrical impulses are then stored on magnetic disks. A disk is made of the same basic material as the tape from a cassette or VCR, only it's in a circular, flat format. Instead of winding by a head that plays the information like a cassette does, it whirls *underneath* the head, like a record or CD. Actually, a disk drive operates exactly the same way as a tape deck does: it records and plays back information. Instead of playing and recording music (which it can do in some cases), a disk drive records the bits directed to it from the microprocessor. When you type in a command on your PC, all the keys send their binary codes to the processor, which quickly adds them together to get you the information you want from the disk. A disk is used because it can be spun around quickly, and all the information is on one flat surface; a tape would have to be wound and rewound to get the right information (although many large computer systems still have tape drives). The disk drive head also moves very quickly, something a stationary tape head doesn't do at all. This helps a disk drive to record and retrieve information at a much higher rate than a tape player.

All this information has to be viewed or heard somehow so that we can make use of it. Up until the 1970s, this information always came out in the form of a paper printout. With the advances made in video displays during the 1970s, computer information is now almost always viewed first on a monitor, which is just a TV tube designed specifically for the computer. Computers have color or monochrome monitors, laser or dot-matrix printers, hard disk drives or floppy disk drives. All of this is something to get into when you look at computers by themselves, but really doesn't apply directly to music and technology.

I will make one comment, though, about disk drives. Floppy disks hold anywhere from 320 kilobytes to 1 megabyte of information, depending on your computer. This is fine when you're starting out, because this much information seems almost overwhelming. However, a hard disk drive holds from 20 to 100 times as much information as a floppy disk, and is much less susceptible to damage from being left on your desk, or from getting Dr. Pepper or gin and tonics spilled on it, or from simple things like fingerprint oil and even dust. For this reason, plus the fact that floppy disk drives require switching different disks in and out of the system, I highly (read *strongly*) recommend getting a hard drive with any computer you buy.

It is also like buying a stereo. Sure, you can start out with 20 watts of power, but it only takes two weeks until you lust after that 80-watt system, and then the 200-watt Monstro Master, and ultimately the 1000-watt Carnegie Hall/L.A. Forum Seismic Stereo Simulator . . . . What can I say? Power corrupts. But having lots of it—in your stereo or in your computer—sure is convenient. And fun.

When thinking of a computer's actual operation, be aware that there are three levels of goings-on. First, there's the hardware, which is the actual, physical machine itself. An IBM, an Apple, an Atari, a Commodore, a Compaq, and a clone are all just pieces of hardware. At this stage, it's essentially the frame of an unwired house. Next comes the operating system. The operating system of a computer is primarily a piece of software that gives the computer the ability to handle the next and last stage of operation, the application. In IBM-type machines, the operating system is separate from the hardware in that it is always necessary to use an operating system disk to get the computer to even understand that it is a computer. This is accomplished by using software designed specifically for the PC such as MS-DOS or OS/2. Each of these types of software is a halfway point to running an application. It's a little different in an Apple, though, where the operating system is an integral part of the hardware, because the Apple hardware and software operating system only understand each other. You can't switch to another operating system on an Apple machine like you can with an IBM. This is also what makes machines like the Apple

Macintosh more popular among novices and casual computer users: the operating system doesn't have its own weird codes and commands like an IBM because it is more directly linked to the hardware. When using DOS or OS/2, you're oftentimes faced with a bewildering array of commands even before you get to your application. The Apple machines eliminate this step.

Finally, you have applications, which turn the computer from an autistic, unknowing machine into an autistic savant. An application is any software package that has a very specific and defined purpose, like a word processor, a database, a drawing package, or a music sequencer. If you think of applications as being specific areas of operation or knowledge, then you realize the computer's true role as an autistic savant. It only does things well that it understands, and usually only one thing at a time. Like Dustin Hoffman's character in the movie *Rain Man,* computers are phenomenal at making calculations, but not at understanding things most people would call "normal." That's why we use strange commands to operate them (the English language is too complex for even the world's most powerful computers to understand), and why they usually only run one application at a time. A computer can understand each of these applications because the software tells it what to do, and also has the machine's undivided attention. That's why you can't write The Great American Novel at the same time that you're composing The World's Greatest All-Time Love Song. An application takes command of a computer system, telling it where to put its 1s and 0s and what to do with them.

A computer system can be described in terms of a house. The hardware is the basic framing of the house, and the framing is what gives the house its shape. Operating systems are like the wiring and plumbing of a house: they determine how and where certain kinds of information will be used. Finally, applications are the actual working parts of the house that extend from the wiring and plumbing. Things like sinks, appliances, air conditioners, faucets, garbage disposals, ovens, and so on are all the parts of the wiring and plumbing that we actually use. But it takes the wiring and plumbing, and before that, the framing, to get us to the point where we can use appliances and running water. All of this works together to form a complete system. You can't operate a microwave out in the middle of the desert, and a house isn't much good with electricity or plumbing. Hence, all three parts are vital to the operation of the computer as a complete system.

That's it. That's all the "advanced technological" information you need to get a grip on what makes computers work the way they do. My father was in the computer business in the 1960s and 1970s, and tried to make this apparent to me for decades. Whenever understanding computers got confusing (which was often), he always boiled it down to one statement: "You only have to remember one thing about understanding how computers work. A computer is all 1s and 0s. That's it. Just those 1s and 0s. If you know that, you know it all. 1s and 0s."

As you finish this chapter, remember 1s and 0s. That's all that matters to a computer. You don't have to know binary code or decimal/binary conversion; the computer already knows all that. The same thing applies to using a car; you know an engine makes it run, you don't need to know the principles of engine combustion to get it to work for you.

All you need to do is be able to start it up and drive it away. As fast and far as *you* want.

4

The Ins and Outs of MIDI

ick up a phone . . . *any* phone. With that phone you can communicate with almost anyone else anywhere in the world. Regardless of the kind of phone they have, regardless of the manufacturer, the country, or the national language, your phone will communicate with their phone. This is known as compatibility.

Standards for international telephone communications were established decades ago, and since then, every equipment vendor and carrier has had to adhere to those standards.

Unfortunately, much of the rest of the world didn't plan ahead as well as the phone industry. The computer business, for example, has been embroiled for years in discussions about how to better network together computers from different manufacturers. A machine from IBM won't talk to or share information with one from Apple. This applies to almost every major computer manufacturer. If someone buys an IBM system, and then wants to hook an Apple Macintosh II up to it, it will hardly be as easy as connecting two different phones. Much money, time, and pulling of hair will be necessary to make such a connection between computers. This is due to product incompatibility.

The same factor held true in establishing formats for videocassette recorders. While Sony tried to convince the world to go with Beta format, and got the jump on the market, other vendors plotted to use the VHS format and convince users to adopt VHS. What happened is now legendary. Since Beta and VHS tapes don't work in VCRs designed for the other medium—because they are incompatible—a lot of people who bought Beta machines found that they were out of luck when the video merchandisers decided to wholeheartedly support VHS.

Other examples of product incompatibility range from diesel engines versus unleaded gasoline engines, on to the standards for the newly developed high-definition television (HDTV), where the U.S. wants one transmission standard, Japan and Europe, another.

Once upon a time, musical synthesizers were trapped in the same kind of debates. Trying to get a few keyboard instruments to work together was impossible because every vendor had their own ideas about getting synths to share information. Why would this even be necessary, you might ask?

THE VERY BRIEF HISTORY OF MUSICAL INSTRUMENT COMMUNICATION ⎯⎯⎯

For the answer, we have to go back to the idea that emerged in the 1970s that the synthesizer could—and oftentimes should—behave like a computer. The outfitting of electronic instruments with microprocessors meant that a wealth of data was being utilized within one instrument. As with computers, what if some of this wealth of information could be shared? As an example, if you were a musician in the 1970s and early 1980s, you might have had a few different synthesizers and drum machines manufactured by different companies. There might have been times when you wanted to have the drum machine keep perfect time with what you were playing on one synthesizer. Or you might have wanted the synthesizer with the great string sounds to play exactly the same thing as what you were playing on the keyboard that had the weird space sounds. If either of these situations, or any of a hundred more, presented itself, you were out of luck, unless you had numerous additional arms and hands at your disposal—not the case with most normally configured humans. It was especially difficult for musicians who played live, simply because only one of a bank of instruments could be used at a time.

Additionally, the desire to synchronize electronic instruments to tape during recording became a driving concern of professional musicians and recording studios, primarily in the use of drum machines. This process of laying down a timing track on tape in order to have synchronization had been used for years in recording soundtracks for TV shows and movies, yet this process was based on specs designed by the video segment of the entertainment industry. With discrepancies in clock times from different manufacturers, the musical segment of the business was having a hard enough time "syncing up" its side of the coin, let alone getting involved with the video side.

A few early concessions were made to intercommunications of equipment, the most notable being the clock output we just mentioned. This device allowed a synthesizer to send a continuous, timed pulse (hence the name "clock") to other instruments, usually a drum machine, which would allow for a certain rudimentary level of synchronization. Unfortunately, the philosophies of music theory and data transmission became confused along the way. Different vendors decided to divide the standard 4/4 time signature into different clock rates. For instance, some manufacturers defined a quarter note with 24 pulses or signals. Others sliced it even thinner, with some vendors using 96 pulses as the indication of a quarter note. Thus, a connection where one synthesizer sent quarter-note information based on 96 pulses to a synthesizer using a 24-pulse system resulted in what can mildly be called "poor timing."

A number of companies began examining ways to curtail this dilemma around 1980. While this was going on, the problem of *inter-manufacturer* communication reared its head. The synthesizer industry was faced with the same prospect of incompatibility that had already cast a shadow over the computer industry.

In a remarkable display of industry unity—for any industry—a group of vendors began work on a proposed specification developed in 1981 by U.S. synth-maker Sequential Circuits. This spec, which was called the Musical Instrument Digital Interface (MIDI), was presented as a combined language/transmission protocol which would not only allow for the sending and receiving of information, but also for determining the structure of that information. During 1982 and 1983, the primary international vendors of keyboard synthesizers—Yamaha, Roland, Sequential Circuits, Kawaii, and Korg—worked at hammering out the physical specifications for the MIDI protocol. Ultimately, they decided on a serial interface, a transmission rate of 31.25K baud (baud is a measure of speed in data communicating), a five-pin DIN connector, and a number of other factors relating to the construction of data messages. Of course, this didn't all happen overnight, and the spec went through a number of incarnations between the initial proposal and the introduction of MIDI Version 1.0-equipped synthesizers in late 1983. Some manufacturers jumped the gun and attempted to beat the spec to market, so a number of instruments were introduced during the summer of 1983 that did not conform to the final published specifications. To combat this kind of "over-eagerness" on the part of vendors, two organizations were formed at the time the spec was completed. The International MIDI Association (IMA) and the MIDI Manufacturers Association (MMA) were set up to serve the needs of the user and the concerns and needs of the manufacturers, respectively. While the IMA kept watch on the sanctity of the MIDI specification, the MMA allowed manufacturers a forum for discussion of critical MIDI issues—primarily that of maintaining compatibility.

COMMERCIAL INTRODUCTION OF MIDI

Mass production of MIDI-equipped instruments began in mid-1984. At that time, the first MIDI software packages for composition, performing, and scoring also appeared. It is important to note here that at no time in the history of the MIDI specification has it become "law"; that is, manufacturers are not legally or even morally bound to adhere to the specification and are free to ignore it if they so desire. However, the motivations of an extremely competitive marketplace have ensured that all vendors want to have all the features that all consumers want, so MIDI has become a de facto requirement for those vendors who plan to make any money in the electronic music business.

The developers of the spec did leave a way out, though, for manufacturers who wanted to add their own bells and whistles to the MIDI standard. Known as a system-exclusive command, this part of the spec allows a manufacturer's machine to transmit unique messages that can only be understood by other machines from that same manufacturer. Although this is still a largely untapped resource in MIDI, it does give manufacturers an outlet within MIDI for "gee-whizzing" their customers. Plus, it's only operable if the user wants to take advantage of it, so it doesn't in any way shut out the normal working benefits of MIDI.

With the exception of the very low end of the market, notably those products that fall into the under-$100 price range, electronic musical equipment, peripherals, and computers all have MIDI capabilities. The extent of those capabilities is varied, with some manufacturers offering more features and more access to MIDI control than others. But one of the best aspects of MIDI is that no matter how fully featured or fully functional the MIDI-equipped device is, it can still be a working part of *any* MIDI system. And if, over time, the MIDI specifications evolve in such a way that the original specs remain compatible with new versions, then MIDI equipment should never become obsolete.

In a day and age when planned obsolescence makes technology replace itself every six months, a system which allows old and new machines to work in tandem for years to come is certainly a welcome innovation. This is particularly true for the millions of consumers who want to invest in and utilize these musical devices without feeling that their investment is going to be worthless in less than a year.

MIDI achieves all of these benefits through the across-the-board implementation of a simple language and transmission protocol, much like the telephone. The following sections will show just how this is done, and how MIDI can be used by the modern musician.

THE IMPORTANCE OF BEING BINARY

Binary code forms the basis of the Musical Instrument Digital Interface just as it is the basis for standard computer equipment. Before we get into bits and bytes—which are the soul of MIDI—let's review the principles of binary calculation. The decimal system relies on multiples of 10. But the binary system requires replacing the columns which are multiples of 10 with columns which are multiples of 2. Thus, there is a ones columns, a twos column, a fours column, an eights column, a sixteens column, a thirty-twos column, a sixty-fours column, and so on. But in place of the 0 through 9 numbers that we used in the decimal system, we now use only the 0 and 1 of the binary system. Hence, numbers (as we think of them decimally) can be represented as binary numbers, which look like 10011001, or 0111, or 1001, or countless other configurations.

Each of these 1s and 0s is not simply called a digit (because they also appear as digits in the decimal system); each is called a *binary digit*. Computer users over the years have shortened the term *binary digit* to *bit*. Every 1 and 0 found in an electronic message is thus known as a bit. But by themselves, a single 1 and a single 0 do not transfer much information.

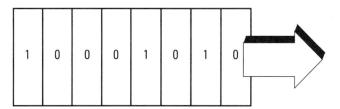

Figure 4-1. One byte composed of eight bits (binary digits).

They are thus combined (in groupings of 2, 4, 6, 8, 16, 32, etc.) into message phrases or words called *bytes* (Fig. 4–1). A byte is a single, complete bit-word; that is, it contains enough 1s and 0s to contain a complete piece of data information. Depending on its structure, a computer's or synthesizer's processor requires a different size word to contain all the important data information. A 16-bit processor can handle a word or byte of up to 16 bits to execute a complete message. The same is true of 8-bit or 32-bit processors utilizing similarly sized bytes to convey information.

WHAT MIDI DOES

MIDI commands are eight-bit messages. There are two different kinds of MIDI messages: one that indicates status (*what* to do) and one that indicates data (the specifics of *how*). Before we discuss the way all of this information streams from place to place and gets used, let's examine exactly what MIDI *does*.

The Musical Instrument Digital Interface is just that—an interface. Its primary function is to allow for communication or networking between two or more electronic instruments. The term "electronic instruments" encompasses many types of music apparatus: keyboards; drum machines; samplers; guitar synthesizers; microcomputers outfitted with a MIDI connection; software for recording, composing, and writing music; as well as hundreds of peripheral effects such as sound enhancers (reverb, chorus, distortion, etc.).

For all of these components to work together, they must be told what is desired by the user. But as has been discussed earlier in these pages, telling multiple machines what to do simultaneously is a feat for which the human body (and sometimes mind) is not built. Connecting all of these components together, however, and controlling them from a master source, is something that humans *can* manage.

When two or more electronic instruments are connected using a MIDI link, the possibilities of control are seemingly endless. MIDI can single out individual synthesizers in a network and tell them when to turn on. It can tell them which notes to play and which to keep silent. It can play one synthesizer in tandem with another, or it can play them in different keys. It can activate drum machines from a master keyboard. It can signal one note to bend up in pitch a whole note, while telling another to bend only a quarter step. It can adjust the tempo of a song in real-time. It can send information to a computer which can then process that information in the same way a tape machine would—with a magnitude more power. It can store and edit specific sound information on computers. It can signal a synthesizer to change from one sound to another when a certain point in a song is played. It can even change sounds for every note of a song.

COMPLETING A MUSICAL DATA LINK

MIDI-equipped instruments have MIDI openings (known as ports) which allow information to be transmitted from one place to another. This works on the same principle as hooking up a cassette player to a stereo amplifier. In order for a cassette deck to play, its output has to be connected to the stereo's input. But to record on the cassette deck using another stereo component (such as phonograph or CD player), the stereo's outputs have to go to the cassette's input, thereby allowing the sound to be sent to the cassette for recording. In this arrangement, there is two-way communication between the amplifier and the cassette deck.

On a MIDI instrument, there are two standard ports, much like on the cassette deck. There is a MIDI OUT port for sending information, and a MIDI IN port for receiving information. In some cases, there is a MIDI THRU port which allows information to keep passing down the line of synthesizers. This port allows for information coming into a synthesizer to be sent on to the next synthesizer as well. This is how multiple instruments can be controlled from a master instrument. (See Fig. 4–2.)

The hookups between all of these ports rely on a single cable of varying lengths, known as a MIDI cable. It contains two connectors—one at each end—which are of the five-pin DIN type. (DIN is a German

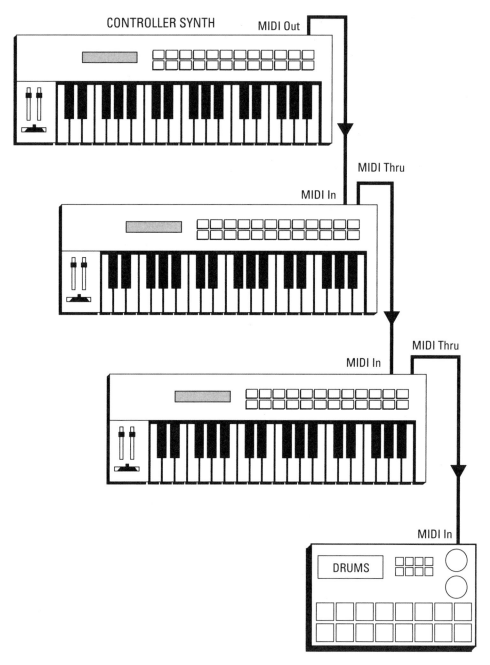

Figure 4–2. Multiple instruments connected by the Musical Instrument Digital Interface (MIDI).

designation referring to ergonomic specifications, which determine how comfortable a component is to use.) This plug fits into any MIDI opening, which means that any cable works with any instrument in any configuration, without the need for a special OUT cable or a special THRU cable. In other words, one size fits all.

MIDI can transmit on any of 16 different channels. This is analogous to your FM radio being able to pick up numerous radio stations. Depending on how you tune it, your radio receives a particular station. The same is true for MIDI messages. You may want to activate a sound on synthesizer number 3 without changing any other synthesizers. Thus, you would set it to a specific MIDI channel separate from the channels that you have assigned to other synthesizers. By the way, the channel number you assign to an instrument is completely up to you, as long as the receiving instrument is set to the same channel. Even if you have just three instruments, you could choose to transmit on channels 9, 10, and 11. The key is that each instrument be set to the proper channel, so that when the master instrument sends out messages for that instrument, they are communicating on the same "wavelength." If the master instrument sends out MIDI messages along channel 9 to synthesizer 3, but synthesizer 3 was set to channel 8, nothing happens. In the world of MIDI connections, this is usually an oversight on the part of the user. We'll explain more about transmitting and receiving later in this chapter.

STATUS AND DATA BYTES

As we mentioned, MIDI messages are divided into status and data information bytes. A status byte (remember, a byte has eight bits) tells the receiving instruments that an action is required. Most often this action is either a "note on" or "note off" command, which is simply a signal to activate or de-activate a particular note. Status bytes are also used to send information on controller modifications to another instrument. Controllers include things like pitch wheels and benders.

Once the status byte is sent, the receiving instrument is alerted to the presence of a new command. The status byte always starts with a 1 in the binary code, so the synth is ready for a brand new piece of information regarding a function. In this first byte, the first four bits tell it to either turn on or turn off a note. That's it. Just turn something on or off. It doesn't tell just what to turn on or off yet. It just prepares the synth for an action. The second four bits of this status byte tell the synth which MIDI channel the action is going to take place on. After the status byte has passed, the receiving instrument knows that an action is going to take place, and on which channel it's going to take place.

Next comes a data byte. This little blast of eight bits will fill in the blanks left by the passing of the status byte. Think of it as being a motorcade. The first thing you see is the police who stop the traffic, indicating that something is going to happen along this particular route of traffic. This happens before you even get to see who's coming up the road. But the presence of the police—definitely a status byte—lets you know that something of importance is coming your way.

Then the data bytes come into view. There are always two, for a total of 16 bits of information. The eight bits in data byte 1 indicate which *actual note* to turn on or off. Actually, the first bit is always a 0, which lets the synth know that it is indeed a data byte. The other seven bits go into creating the number which designates a specific keyboard position. Thus, it begins to fill in the information signaled by the status byte. This data byte may signal the A# an octave above middle C, or any other note on the keyboard, all of which are assigned a place in binary coding.

Then comes data byte 2, which tells the receiving instrument *how* the note is to be played. This involves key velocity, which is an indication of how hard or how soft a key is hit. In the most up-to-date keyboards, the pressure of a finger on the key, as well as how fast or slow it is hit, register different MIDI messages. For instance, hitting a key very hard may make the sound louder *and* activate a significant part of the sound. If, say, a trumpet sound is being used, and the key is hit lightly, it may produce only a light, even trumpet tone. But if it is hit with greater force, the trumpet sound may also have some raspiness to it, much as if a trumpeter were forcing a lot of air through the instrument. These kinds of messages are contained in data byte 2. (See Fig. 4–3.)

That's the basic motorcade. The police show up, thereby alerting you that something is happening on this particular street. Then you get to see what it is that's actually happening in the motorcade. It may be the President or the Pope in the first car, and the Vice President in the second car (he always has the less important role). Or it may be a funeral with two hearses

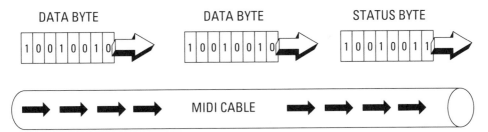

Figure 4-3.   One MIDI message, containing a status byte and two data bytes.

or two ambulances. It might even be something as mundane as two of those wide-load trucks that take up the whole street. You get the picture.

In all, there are three parts to one single MIDI message. Part One is the status byte, alerting the receiving instrument to an impending action (like the police). Part Two is the first data byte, which indicates the particular of what is going on (like the President's car). Part Three is the second data byte, used to make sure that the proper conditions are applied to the first data byte (*exactly* like the Vice President's car). MIDI message number one is complete.

However, it takes an incredible number of these messages to make up a discernible piece of music. Not only does this procedure have to be used to turn individual notes on, but it has to be used to turn them off (which happens very soon after they are turned on), to indicate the sound to be used for that note, and to indicate modifications made to the sound. To make matters more complex, it has to do this for dozens of notes per minute, or in the case of the exceptional keyboardist using all ten fingers, maybe upwards of a thousand times per minute. So these MIDI messages are whipping back and forth from instrument to instrument *one after the other* to communicate all of this information.

THE RACE TO RECEIVE

This may seem a bit like a relay race, and it is. The MIDI protocol uses serial transmission, which transmits one piece of information at a time. There are other forms of electronic communication which are faster, notably parallel, but this was deemed too expensive by the original MIDI specifiers, who didn't think the additional speed was worth the price, especially for consumer instruments. So the information is transmitted in a line and, as can be imagined, this has to happen very quickly.

Transmission rates are known as *bauds* (sounds like "bods"). Originally used to quantify the pulses per second of telegraph messages, the term comes from a French inventor of the late 1800s named J. M. Baudot. Today, baud rates help to define how fast information in the form of bits is being sent by an electronic device. In the computer industry, the standard rates of transmission are 300, 600, and 1200 baud. For 1200 baud, the rate of transmission is about 120 eight-bit words per second. In comparison, the average person converses at somewhere between 120 to 160 words per minute, or two to three words per second. Thus, normal speaking is about $1/60$th to $1/40$th as slow as normal data transmission rates. At a rate of 31,250 baud, MIDI transmits the equivalent of 3125 8-bit words per second. That's enough to handle almost anything that can be sent down the wire in real-time. But the operative word is almost.

Given the number of instruments that can be connected or linked in a MIDI network (limited only by expense), distance starts to play a factor in the speed of data transmission. In the computer industry, the only thing slowing transmission speeds is the speed of light, because microprocessor activities take place in such a close proximity—measured in microns—that any more closeness would cause them to burn from electrical friction. But in a MIDI set-up, the distance from synth to synth starts causing a slowdown in the system after about four synths. This is because the information must travel the length of the cables, whip through the internals of interspersed synths, and make it to the final destination. Signal degradation takes place in any electrical system where long distances must be travelled. Couple this with a piece of music that may have almost one thousand notes per minute, with everything from pitch bending to the kitchen sink thrown in, and one can understand the limits of the MIDI transmission spec.

However, this latter instance is not the norm, and MIDI data speed seems to be suitable for all but the most data intense applications. So once all this data is running around at 3125 bytes of information per second, how does the receiving instrument know how to distinguish messages meant for it versus information meant for another receiving instrument? Good question, and one that leads us right into the heart of MIDI control of specific instruments: the MIDI modes.

MIDI MODES

The modes in MIDI refer to the channel selection and internal workings of the receiving instruments. There are four modes, and they are comprised of the various pairings of three concepts: OMNI, POLY, and MONO.

OMNI refers, like the word "omniscient," to everything and everywhere. This message comes in two formats: OMNI ON and OMNI OFF. In the OMNI ON format, a receiving synthesizer will accept every bit of information that is sent from the master synth, regardless of channel. When the OMNI OFF format is employed, the receiving synth receives only messages on the channel it is set to. If it is set to channel 4, and a message for channel 7 comes down the cable, the synth ignores it. OMNI ON is like a broken dam—everything comes washing in and is used by the synth—whereas OMNI OFF is a controlled flow that directs water through specific water pipes. When a receiving synth is in the OMNI ON mode, it is standing in front of the dam waiting for everything, come what may. In OMNI OFF, it picks a water pipe and stands in front of that, waiting for water that comes only out of that pipe. Thus, OMNI refers to specifically channel considerations.

Next is the idea of POLY, or polyphonic. "Polyphonic" is a term used to describe synthesizers that can play more than one note at a time. Although this sounds like a pretty obvious given, synthesizers did not always possess this ability. Originally, the large and small synthesizers of the 1960s and 1970s had one thing in common, which was that they could only emit sound for one note at a time, or monophonically. The inner workings of those synths were so cumbersome that all available resources went into producing and then modifying individual tones. With the advent of polyphonic synths in the late 1970s, the monophonic synth went the way of the dinosaur. However, there is still a warm spot in the hearts of old synth users and developers, and so the concept of POLYphony is still kept separate from that of MONOphony. An interesting result of trying to play chords on a monophonic keyboard is that the instrument usually chooses notes based on when fingers depress the keys. So whichever finger of a five-finger chord hits the monophonic keyboard first, that is the note that is usually generated.

The concepts of POLY and MONO, when combined with the concepts of OMNI ON and OMNI OFF, give us the four MIDI modes: OMNI ON/ POLY, OMNI ON/MONO, OMNI OFF/POLY, and OMNI OFF/MONO.

All of these are set by the user on the receiving instrument. These modes are fairly diverse, so it is necessary to look at each one in detail.

OMNI ON/POLY is Mode 1. In this particular configuration, everything that comes from the master synth is played by the receiving instrument—everything. Regardless of channel and number of notes per chord, the OMNI ON/POLY setting assures that no matter what the master generates, it will be received and replayed by the receiving synth.

OMNI ON/MONO is Mode 2. This setting, which is not employed often, allows for all information being sent from the master to be received by the slave instrument, *but* this information will be played monophonically. Thus, full chords being sent on channels 1 thru 16 will be received, but the receiving synth will then have to decide which notes to be played. Again, it often chooses the one note of a chord which is depressed first. Variations involve the receiving synth choosing the highest or lowest note of a chord.

OMNI OFF/POLY is Mode 3. This is one of the more frequently employed modes because it allows a synth to play polyphonically, but only on selected channels. Therefore, if a sequence of chords is sent down channel 6 by the master synth, the receiving instrument must also be set to channel 6 in order to actually play those chords. This goes back to the analogy of standing in front of a specific water pipe and waiting for the flow from that pipe only. Thus, chords can be played, but only when the proper channel is assigned.

OMNI OFF/MONO is Mode 4. Contrary to how this sounds, it doesn't limit the synthesizer to one specific channel and one specific note at a time, although that is the basis of the concept. What this does allow the user to do is configure the receiving single keyboard as if it were multiple monophonic keyboards. Thus, each of these "individual" keyboard settings is able to receive monophonic information on a specific channel. At first this may sound like a difficult way to achieve OMNI OFF/POLY, or Mode 3. In effect, that is what this mode resembles, *if* the synthesizer is a *single*-timbral instrument. Single-timbral instruments can only play one *sound* at a time over the length of the keyboard. Anytime a sound is changed, that change affects all the notes on the keyboard. A multi-timbral instrument, on the other hand, allows the user to divide up the keyboard to employ multiple sounds at once. On a *multi*-timbral instrument, the user's left hand may be playing a cello sound while the right hand is playing a flute sound. Usually, the divisions can be made even more specific, so that a keyboard may be able to play six or eight different sounds at once.

This latter possibility is where the potential of the OMNI OFF/MONO lies. A multi-timbral synth on the receiving end could very well take in six or eight different channels of monophonic playing, and then assign them simultaneously to different sounds. If polyphony is desired, the user can set three or four channels to the same sound, so that the individual notes from those channels are layered to form chords. Then the remaining channels can be used as solo sounds.

OTHER MIDI FEATURES

There are a number of other neat features of MIDI that you can use the more familiar you become with the technology. We will briefly describe some of them next.

Program Change

This is one part of MIDI transmission that doesn't deal specifically with notes, because it deals with sounds. Well, the selection of sounds, anyway. Every time you change a patch on your synth, that is known technically as a program change, because you're changing from one sound program (patch) to another one. Using MIDI, program changes can be activated from a master controller or a sequencer without ever physically touching the instrument that you want to change the sound patch on. A MIDI program change sends out information about (1) which MIDI channel is to change (thereby affecting any instrument on that channel) and (2) which patch/program to change to. This is an especially powerful feature if you are sequencing a number of synths or sound modules together, and you want them to change to different sounds at different times throughout your piece. Putting program changes into the sequence keeps you from having to leap around your setup (like Keith Emerson and Rick Wakeman used to do) pushing patch buttons every time a sound needs to change. It gives you the freedom to sit back and listen to your musical work while the system automatically makes those patch changes for you.

Control Change

Control change works on the same principle as program change, only it affects things like volume control, foot pedal control, pressure control, and the modulation wheel. These are all peripherals that control certain functions on a particular synth. Their performance levels (exactly how much sustain, the range that the mod wheel covers, etc.) can be defined using MIDI, and they can also be changed without physically touching the synths that they control—like a program change command.

System Exclusive

This is one of the most unusual features of the MIDI specification. It allows for manufacturers to send commands between instruments that will only be recognized by other instruments from that same manufacturer. Hence, the term refers to information that is exclusive to a particular type of system. This command is used primarily for sending patch information between two synths or sound modules from the same manufacturer, a function which allows musicians to swap internal patch data between two machines using MIDI. This command is also used for sending out information along a MIDI network—again, mostly when a *sequencer* is at work. The sequencer (see Chapter Eight) can send out information so that only XYZ's machines respond to the command, but ABC's machines don't.

Song Position

This is a command sent out from MIDI drum machines and sequencers that tells all the other MIDI instruments where they are supposed to be at a certain point in time. As the song progresses—using either the drum machine or sequencer as the master song clock—these devices send out continuous information about how many beats have already passed during the course of the song. This allows other instruments to "jump on" to the song at precise beats (like catching the pole on a merry-go-round as it spins around). Another helpful feature that keeps everything in sync.

Song Select

If a sequencer or drum machine has stored a number of songs in memory, those songs can be specifically recalled by sending a song select command from another device. Like the program change, it keeps the musician from having to push all kinds of buttons to select the particular song that is to be played. As long as the song is programmed with a particular number, it can be retrieved automatically within a MIDI system.

USING MIDI TECHNOLOGY

This is all well and good, but what is one supposed to *do* with all of this MIDI technology? Good question . . . and one that has an even better answer. Although we'll look at specifics in later chapters, let's examine some of the options available via MIDI and MIDI-equipped components for three distinct scenarios: the individual musician, the studio environment, and live performance. Each of these environments can make use of MIDI in unique ways.

The Individual Musician

Looking at the benefits of MIDI from the standpoint of the individual, let's create a situation where only one person—say, a keyboard player (although it could be a drummer or guitarist or flutist or other musician)—is confronted with exploring the vast potential of MIDI. This person has a keyboard, a drum machine, a computer, some software, and a standard stereo cassette deck. Without access to any other musicians, this keyboard player would like to compose a song, but is limited by his or her ability to play only the keyboard, and the fact that your basic cassette recorder will only record one session at a time; it cannot be overdubbed or multitracked. This is because it only has one recording head, which allows for stereo input, but only at one time—you can record two input devices at the same time, but you can't record one and *then* the other at two different times.

Without MIDI, the computer and its software don't even figure into the loop here. There is no means of transmitting data from instrument to computer, from computer to instrument, or even from computer to tape deck (some personal computers now offer an "audio out" jack, although computers didn't do much more than bleep and buzz up until about 1987). So, in a sense, the keyboard player in this situation has a number of disparate elements that don't do anything together. Sort of like a room filled with a telephone, a dictionary, and a turbo-charged V-8 engine.

They're all useful in their own right, but don't necessarily belong together.

Enter MIDI. The keyboard player can plug his synthesizer into a MIDI adapter for the computer. This is done by adding a special card to the computer, just as a modem or color-screen adapter would be added to allow for access to telephone lines or color monitors. With the proper software, usually referred to as sequencing or compositional software, the computer becomes the digital equivalent of multitrack tape deck. Sequencing software allows the musician to operate the computer as a recorder, and provides multiple tracks that the musician can record different parts on. For instance, Track One may be the rhythm part, while Track Two is the melody or lead section. The keyboard player can record the two tracks, or even more if necessary, at separate times, and with the proper software can even go directly into the computer, via its typewriter keyboard, to correct mistakes.

This is all possible because the recording is not actually of sound, but of digital representations of the actions made on the keyboard that create that sound. So instead of actually recording the *sound* of a piano rhythm and a trumpet melody line, the computer is just storing the representation of those sounds. Going into the computer to fix a missed note doesn't result in changing the trumpet note to another appropriate trumpet note; it changes the data note to another data note. Thus, actual sound is not affected by this editing. It is not even affected by speeding up or slowing down the tempo of the music on the computer, because such changes only affect how quickly the data moves, not how quickly the sound moves. On a tape deck, the sound is in hard form—meaning it has a physical presence on a strip of tape. Speeding up that tape results in higher-pitched sounds. However, in a digital system, the information is speeded up before it gets to the sound, meaning the actual sound isn't affected at all. Changes are made before the sound within the synth even has to do its job. (The exception to this is digital sampling, which performs the same function as a tape, but the physical form of the sound is digital, not analog. Sampling affects the actual sound, as opposed to how the sound is used, which is one of MIDI's functions.)

Indeed, there is no sound coming from the computer *at all*. It is simply a repository for data. Only when it is hooked up to a sound "maker," such as a synth or drum machine, can the computer produce sounds. This is hard to visualize, since all of the data is physically stored on the computer, but there are a number of ways to understand the concept. A V-8 engine creates energy and thrust, but it doesn't *go* anywhere if it isn't attached to a chassis with wheels. For all its power, it remains stationary unless it is linked to some movable apparatus, like wheels on an axle. The same is true of radio and TV signals. These invisible signals are sent out into the air every second of every 24 hours of every day, and pass unnoticed through the room you're sitting in, or the chair you're sitting on, and even through your body. Yes, even as you read this, the local FM rock station, the AM news station, and reruns of *Gilligan's Island* are passing harmlessly through your body. But your body isn't a receiver, and it can't translate the signal data into sounds or television pictures. Only radios and TVs are designed to receive the data and then turn it into music or visual images.

The computer works the same way with the synth, sending data that is then translated into sounds in a sequence to produce music. The musician now has two tracks (or more, if so desired) of information simultaneously coming out of his computer into the synth, whereas before, the only sound coming out of the synth was what his or her two hands could manage to play at once. But the synth can now be connected to the drum machine to activate that instrument in synchronization with the computer. Since the computer has recorded the tracks of the song with a tempo, that tempo is then sent back to the synth, with commands to keep everything in time. The time message—not the sound or key data—can then be passed on to the drum machine at the same time to keep it in sync with the overall operation. Now the keyboard player has three specific song parts being played by the computer; the rhythm, the melody line, and the drum sounds. All of these are audible—provided they are amplified or accessed with headphones—and constitute a fairly complete ensemble performance created by the one musician, the lone keyboard player.

The outputs of both the synth and the drum machine can then be directed to the two input channels of the tape deck, where a single recording will record all three parts in harmony with each other. This is possible because the drum machine is producing one part while the one keyboard is producing two parts. The use of adapters, junctions, and Y-cords would allow for even more inputs of music from more synths and other sound-producing components.

As a final bonus to the individual composer, much of the sequencing software available today can print out the composition in notational form. This notational form is yet another representation of the MIDI data that was put into the computer, and can be viewed as a complete score of the song, including time signatures, measures, accidentals, ties, beams, and an array of other notational necessities. Not only does the musician now have a three-part recording of the song, but also has the complete printed score —without ever setting pen to paper. It's enough to give a single musician a taste of what it's like to be the Supreme Being. This is what happens when you exert complete control over the creative process.

The Studio Environment

When bands like the Beatles and Led Zeppelin recorded their first albums (each done within one week's time), 4-track recording was the accepted method of laying down album tracks, and 8- and 16-track recordings were pushing the ceiling of technology. Today, even garage bands scoff at having less than 16 tracks to play with, and 24 tracks is the norm. But the change from the primitive recording methods of the 1960s to the highly digitized methods of the 1980s and 1990s has resulted in an almost anachronistic situation: Digital production has lost some of the "warmth" or "ambience" of those heavily overdubbed and multimicrophoned recordings of two decades ago. Digital methodology has eliminated the messiest factor of those recordings—noise, hiss, unwanted room sounds—but some of the fullness and depth of the sounds in those recordings has been lost in the process as well.

By MIDIing a number of instruments together, much of this sound ambience can be recaptured. For instance, taking the grand piano sound patches from two different manufacturers and connecting them via MIDI creates one grand piano sound that is much more lush than either of the individual sounds by themselves. And the addition of a MIDI-equipped peripheral effects, such as a digital reverb or chorus unit, allows ambience and depth to be reinserted into digital sounds, without adding the noise that comes from microphoning the acoustic versions of those sounds.

Cost-effectiveness and even cost reduction in the studio environment can be achieved with MIDI as well. Since MIDI is standardized in all instruments and environments, much of the time-consuming and dollar-eating aspects of the studio can be accomplished by musicians in the comfort of their own homes. Things like pre-production or laying down synthesizer tracks can be performed and perfected before a musician even steps into a high-priced recording studio. A musician can bring a floppy disk of the sequences in his or her pocket into the studio and lay down the tracks in near-finished form by inserting the disk into the studio computer. This is not meant to take anything away from professional studios, which have more equipment for turning out quality recordings than most musicians can even imagine. Yet the availability of MIDI as a standard allows musicians of any financial stratum to do much of the grueling recording basics in a familiar setting, and then utilize that same work as a basis for more extensive recording in a professional studio.

From the view of the studio engineer and other studio personnel, MIDI allows for the automation of certain tasks that can either be monotonously time-consuming or mind-numbingly repetitive. The musician who continually screws up the one passage in a song can have parts—indeed, individual notes—edited and corrected if MIDI sequencing is utilized. This minimizes the number of times that a tape has to be rewound in order to accommodate the musician. One MIDI recording may be all that is necessary to eliminate wasted and valuable studio time. There are also specific recording functions which are separate from the musician that can be controlled via MIDI. The activation of certain effects, the automating of mixing levels and other mixing board functions, and the synchronization of instruments are all tasks that can be relegated to MIDI components in varying degrees.

MIDI also allows for easier scoring and tracking of music to video works. MIDI data, once recorded, can be synchronized to video or movie tape by electronically linking it up with SMPTE code, which is the video industry's timing specification. SMPTE stands for Society of Motion Picture and Television Engineers, and is a long-time standard that is the movie and TV equivalent of MIDI. A number of devices exist which can automatically sync up MIDI music and SMPTE video cues in the studio (see the discussion of clock pulses on page 37), thereby eliminating that anxious moment when a musician has to strike the proper note . . . right . . . about . . . NOW! When it's missed, the tape has to be rewound, and the part comes up again until it's done right. With MIDI, much of the guesswork is reduced, if not altogether eliminated. That's why someone like Jan Hammer can score *Miami Vice* all by himself, or Stewart Copeland can score Saturday morning cartoons with an extreme degree of efficiency on a weekly basis.

In almost any other environment, musicians cope with mistakes made while playing. Musicians are allowed hundreds of bad notes in their own homes, and even concert presentations are forgiven the occasional glitched note. But in the studio, precision counts more than it does in any other music environment. Not only does it count more, it is expected and demanded. MIDI helps in getting the technicalities of recording closer to perfection by facilitating many aspects of the studio recording process and minimizing the randomness that results in mistakes.

Live Performance

In any live situation, a musician is even more severely limited in the number of parts that can be played than he or she is in any compositional or studio setting. Playing live means that the audience gets to see music as a real-time productive process. As we've seen, with only two arms and two legs, musicians are limited to what they can do at any specific time with the instruments at hand. A performer playing in front of 20,000 people cannot ask the audience to sit through one section of music (the rhythm, for instance), and once that is completed, ask them to then listen to the melody line, and then ask them to fuse the two together mentally to appreciate the whole composition. No, the live performer has to try to duplicate the recorded structures of a piece all together with *less* opportunity in concert to actually produce them all. The luxury of a studio allows a musician the time and the resources to clone himself or herself many times over. A live situation only allows for the presentation of one part: the one the performer delivers in front of the audience's eyes. Obviously, a four-piece band that laid down 24 tracks on their latest studio album can only reproduce four of those tracks in their entirety live.

MIDI, because of its ability to link different instruments and trigger sound sources at set points in time, gives the performer much of the "self-cloning" capability that he or she has at home or in the studio. There are obvious possibilities here, notably linking a number of synthesizers so that one keyboard player can activate many sounds simultaneously. But live, other MIDI routes to duplicating studio recordings become possible. A guitar player can utilize a guitar synth in concert so that both the true electric guitar sound and a specific synth sound (or six separate synth sounds, one for each string) are audible while he or she is playing one instrument. The guitarist can have only the lowest bass string activated so that it sounds a bass synth sound each time it is plucked, in addition to sounding a standard electric guitar tone. A drummer can set up a specific MIDI-equipped drum so that when it is struck it activates a synth connection. This might trigger only one sound, or perhaps a series of sounds, such as a spoken effect, or a preprogrammed sequence of notes and sounds (Fig. 4–4).

This type of set-up was adopted around 1986–1987 by rock trios such as Emerson, Lake & Powell and Rush, both of which had taken full advantage of 24-track studios for their albums released during that time period. Reproducing those albums with any degree of accuracy—some might say similarity—required the MIDIing of dozens of additional instruments to the instruments that the performers manipulated on stage. The audience

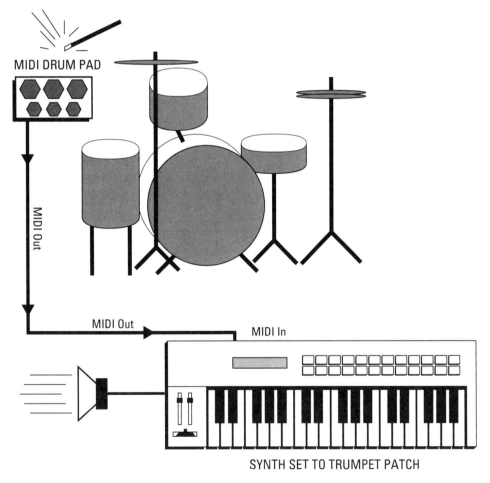

Figure 4-4.   MIDI drum pad activating synthesizer patch; each strike on pad activates a synth "trumpet" patch.

still saw the three performers playing their respective instruments with the usual concert fervor, but did not see the banks and racks of synth components which resided off-stage responding to the musicians' MIDI commands. And during live performance, instruments can be MIDI-triggered by the instrument at hand, by foot pedals, or even by computers synchronized to the ongoing performance. This is a testimony not only to the possible scope and implementation of MIDI functions during concert, but also to a musician's ability to utilize every limb and extremity in order to maximize the effect of a live performance.

There is an additional area where MIDI can have an impact on a live show: lighting and staging. Manufacturers make lighting systems which can be turned on and off, adjusted for color and intensity, and manipulated in every conceivable manner by MIDI commands. Again, a specific note or specific instrument, as well as a computer or other MIDI device, can activate the control of these lights. The same is true of adjusting certain sound levels, or triggering stage effects that rely on synchronization with a particular downbeat or a swell in a piece of music. Thus the drummer, in addition to playing drums and activating synthesizer sequences, may be serving as the light person and special effects controller, and carrying out these functions *all at the same time.* It becomes clear that the potential of MIDI can give musicians control over more aspects of a stage presentation than was ever possible in the past.

This concludes our overview of the Musical Instrument Digital Interface and its importance in music. All of the information in this chapter concerns what MIDI is, how it works, and how it came to be. In subsequent chapters, we will look at the specific relevance of MIDI in applications from composition to recording to performing, on to training and education.

Like the telephone, MIDI has allowed people—specifically musicians—to be in places they can't be and accomplish creative tasks they couldn't do otherwise. For today's musician, MIDI is the next best thing to being there.

5

Synthesizers

he machine that changed the entire face of music technology is the venerable synthesizer. Since its creation in the high-tech research labs of the United States and Europe in the late 1950s and early 1960s, the synthesizer has come to define the term "electronic musical instrument" more than any other musical instrument.

We are all somewhat familiar with synthesizers, whether or not we play an instrument. Apart from the electric guitar, the synthesizer is the most pervasive electronic instrument in popular music. Just about every radio station—whether the format is Contemporary Hits Radio (CHR), Middle of the Road (MOR), New Age, or Album Oriented Rock (AOR)—features music that uses synths. From heavy metal to light pop to jazz to "ambient" music, today's sounds generally have a synthesizer plugging along in some capacity. Often we immediately recognize synthesizers as synthesizers: strange droning sounds that aren't at all natural, or a spacey string section that doesn't quite sound like strings, but it doesn't sound like anything else, either. At other times, we can't tell a synth from a real instrument, such as a cathedral organ or a whistle, because the synthesist has chosen to re-create those sounds and mimic the actual instruments as closely as possible. Like a cubic zirconium stone that is mistaken for a diamond, a finely crafted synth sound might even be able to fool the experts as to whether or not it's the real thing.

We know the synth by its sounds, and we also know it by sight: it looks like a compressed piano with lots of lights and buttons on it, and almost 100 percent of the time, it's jet-black in color. Most synths actually look like something Darth Vader would have created if he were tired of banging around on real pianos. And like Darth Vader, these machines look pretty intimidating to the uninitiated—sleek black slabs of molded high-tech plastic with flickering green and red lights, and often a small, barely readable screen that conveys written information from little illuminated yellow or blue panels. Add sliding faders and pitch bends, along with programming tools, and you have something that looks more at home on the set of *Star Wars* than on a brightly lit stage, or in somebody's bedroom.

This immediately recognizable instrument has pervaded—and occasionally dominated—the music business since its arrival over two decades ago. But even though we seem to know this instrument, one question seems to linger: *How* does it make all those sounds? What makes all those cool noises? Where do they come from? Why does one synthesizer sound different from another? How, what, when, where, why—and yet again—why? This is the chapter that tells you just about everything you wanted to know about the creation of synthesized sounds. Maybe more.

I am not going to get technical on you; that's the business of the people who make these things. Babe Ruth didn't manufacture baseball bats, but he sure knew how to put them to good use. The same applies here—a little knowledge will give you more control over the synthesizer, without your having to learn how to wave solder-printed circuit boards and program in machine code at the microprocessor level (this is *exactly* the kind of techno-jargon I'll avoid in the following pages).

There are a number of different methods of creating sounds from a synthesizer, most of them being less than ten years old. The easiest way to examine them, then, is to try and take a look at synth technologies as they burst on the scene. Incidentally, contrary to my commitment to give as broad a description of each technology as possible without singling out particular products, describing synths is going to require naming names. This is because many innovations in synth technology were brought to light with the introduction of specific instruments. Those instruments have become standards or prime examples of a specific technology, and we can best point out their differences by discussing the products themselves.

As discussed in Chapter Two, synths were given birth at places like Bell Labs and various universities by people like Robert Moog, Donald Buchla, and Alan R. Pearlman. The names are important because the first synths bore the names of their creators (The Moog, Mini-Moog, and the ARP Series), but the technology employed is much more important. Each of these original and unique innovators found ways to shape and modify electricity so that it could ultimately produce sound that we can describe as "musical." Let's see just how electricity was—and is—made to do our musical bidding.

THE JOY OF VOLTAGE CONTROL

The first synthesizers relied on the generation of a single electronic tone to produce sounds. If you didn't think that electricity produced tones, listen to the noise from a shorted-out music cable that connects an electric instrument to an amplifier. Or listen to a television in a quiet room with the sound turned all the way down. In the first case, you hear an annoying low-frequency hum from the amp; in the second, you hear an almost inaudible high-frequency pitch that emanates from the TV. Both are cases of electricity generating sound.

In the case of synthesizers, a single tone needed to be produced that could then be modified in order to change the resulting "sound." This was done by using an *oscillator*. An oscillator is simply a device that produces a continuous electronic frequency or tone through oscillation. Oscillation is another term for rapid movement or vibration; the oscillator moves at very high speeds and produces a vibration of electricity, which in turn generates a specific tone. In technical terms, this tone is called a regularly repeating waveform. The frequency diagrams in Chapter One show waveforms that do not change with time; they are regularly repeated. Although most natural sounds are not even close to being this pure in nature (no timbres, fading, or variations), it is easy to produce this type of clean, constant tone with an electrical circuit—by using an oscillator.

A constant tone looks like a sine wave. The length of time that a sine wave stretches out before it repeats is how its frequency is determined (Fig. 5–1).

Multiples of this frequency are its harmonics or overtones. If you have a frequency at 440 Hz (the length of one complete cycle), you have the pitch A. If you divide that in half, you double this frequency to 880 Hz, or the next highest A; if you cut it in half to 220 Hz, you have the next lowest A. Dividing this number by other whole numbers (like 3 or 5) give us resulting harmonics. This goes for every single frequency, which gives us all of our different notes and their harmonics. Additionally, no oscillator is completely "pure," meaning that along with the primary frequency it

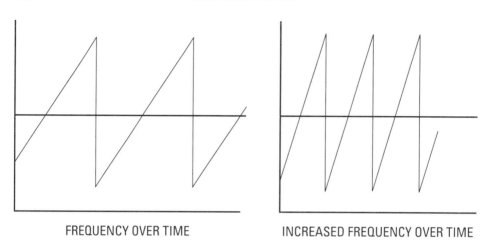

FREQUENCY OVER TIME   INCREASED FREQUENCY OVER TIME

Figure 5-1.   Variation in frequency.

is generating—or is intended to generate—it also produces overtones or harmonics. In any oscillator-produced sound, these overtones contribute to the overall tone. Addition or subtraction of these overtones has a lot of bearing on what the final sound will be like. We'll get to this in a moment when we discuss filters.

A very quick aside: the pitch A is currently equal to 442 Hz. Although originally set at 440 Hz, its frequency was raised by a council in Europe a few decades ago to get a brighter sound out of tunable instruments. This was due to audience demand for more lively sounding musical pieces. Some orchestras actually tune to a higher frequency despite the international standard. There is currently a debate within the world's classical music community about whether to return A to its original 440 status, or to raise it even higher to suit more modern tastes, perhaps as high as 446. If that should happen, what we know as A today may sound closer to what we know as an A# in the future. Don't worry about it, though—nobody will tell anybody else, and we'll probably never know the difference anyway.

An oscillator produces a repeating electrical tone, which equals a specific frequency, which equals a specific note. But to get a different note, like going from an A to a D, we have to change the frequency. This is done by changing the oscillation. Oscillators can be changed by changing the voltage being pumped into them—change the voltage and you change the oscillator, thereby changing the frequency. An oscillator of this sort is called a voltage-controlled oscillator or VCO. VCOs are the most important part of early synth workings. Without a changing oscillator, all you could get is one tone, which makes for some very boring musical production, and it rules out any good solos.

An oscillator producing a straight tone creates a sine wave. This too can become boring and downright tedious after a time. A sine wave yields an even tone that is relatively free of any particular sound characteristics. To add greater variety to the initial sound produced by a VCO, synth developers created circuits that would chop sine waves into other waveforms, specifically sawtooth waves and square (or rectangular) waves. These waveforms are variations of sine waves, and thus easily created by oscillators with a little help from modifier circuits. A sawtooth wave (which is a fundamental sine wave and its *integral* harmonics at a fixed ratio) sounds similar to a bowed violin string (bright, but not very exciting), while a square wave (which is a fundamental sine wave with its *odd-numbered* harmonics at a fixed ratio) produces an almost clarinet-like sound (mellow and perhaps a little hollow). Each of these waveforms gave the original synths a starting point from which to create sounds.

Now that the synthesizer's oscillators produced the frequency part of a waveform, other devices were needed to address shape and amplitude, or timbre and loudness. This meant acting upon the initial waveform to produce tonal variety.

Controlling the shape of a waveform was performed through the use of filters. Electronic filters do just what every other kind of filter in the world does—keeps some things out while allowing others to continue on. Water filters allow water to pass through while keeping out certain impurities like dirt, coffee filters allow water and small coffee particles to pass without allowing larger and undesirable grinds to pass, air filters keep larger particles of dust and dirt out of the air; you get the point. On another level, TVs and radios use electronic filters to focus on a specific station or channel while keeping others out. Synthesizer filters work on the same principle as all of these.

When a tone passes from the VCO into the filter, it arrives as a relatively clear and constant version of a particular waveform, along with a number of normally occurring harmonics. It already has some semblance of timbre, as determined by the shape of the waveform. But in order to get more variations out of the tone, to make it more colorful or distinct or attractive, a filter is used to further shape the waveform. What it actually does is slice portions of the frequency (or frequencies) away from the tone to alter the waveshape. Earlier we saw the simple differences of sound between a sawtooth and square wave, and the process of filtering produces an even more radical variation in the timbres of sounds.

Filters are set to different levels to provide different kinds of tonal coloration, slicing off certain parts of specific frequencies, and eliminating certain harmonic frequencies. Eliminating low frequencies creates a brighter tone, cutting out the higher frequencies makes a much deeper and heavier sound. Again, having just one level of filter would only produce one type of timbre or affect only one frequency, so filters are also controlled by applying voltage to them. This gives us voltage-controlled filters or VCFs. These little filters, working on sounds produced by little oscillators, give us the sounds that produce music in synths. It is because of filters, which subtract parts of the frequency, that most analog synthesis is known as *subtractive synthesis*.

Following right behind the oscillators and filters (which are the number one and two most important parts of your synth, respectively) comes part three, the amplifier. This is not the stack of Marshalls or the concert sound system that you plug your instrument into. It is an internal amplifier for boosting the signal to a strong enough level so that it can be sent out to an external device. Internal amplifiers are known primarily as VCAs. If you haven't caught on by now, and I'm sure that you have, VCA stands for voltage controlled amplifier. Just don't confuse any of these with VCRs, VHF, VHS, and you'll be okay.

These three components make up the basis for all early analog synthesizers (Fig. 5–2). Without them, there is no synthesizer. But we still have a few more steps to look at in order to view the whole synthesizer process, since sound creation is just the essence of synths, not the total environment. An analogy might be wine. Wine is made of grapes, but wine production also involves other processes like aging, temperature control, and storage in certain kinds of casks. Together—these processes and the grapes—make up a fine wine.

Remember what I said earlier about sound being "time-bound"? All sound, especially sound made into music, has time as an integral and inextricable component. Part Four of synthesizer sound production is control over time. We already have our waveforms, but so far they stay pretty constant over time. They are produced (VCO), they are modified (VCF), and they are boosted (VCA), but where is the decay, the fading, or even a level of build-up from soft to loud, or loud to soft? How about the sharpness of

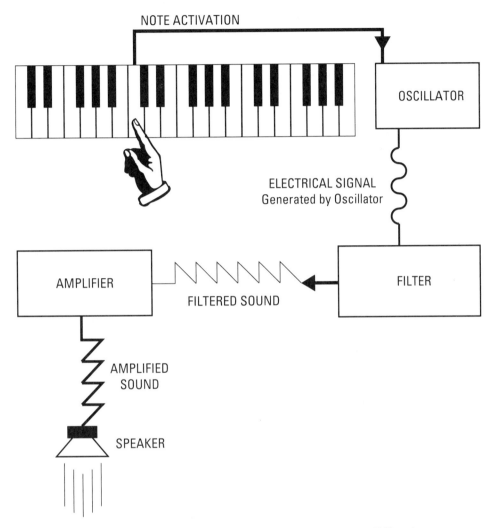

Figure 5–2.   Sound generation, filtering, and amplification.

starting and stopping? These are all time variables not accounted for or handled by all the voltage-controlled devices.

ENVELOPE GENERATORS

Sounds in nature constantly rise and fall in intensity, and also start and stop with a particular intensity. These are factors which change over time, and are not features of a device which produces a constant tone, like a VCO. Therefore, time parameters must be added to the tone produced by a synth. This is done with something called an *envelope generator.*

An envelope generator controls the synthesizer sound over time. An envelope itself is the time pattern of a sound, which consists of attack, delay, sustain, and release. This time function is popularly referred to as simply *ADSR,* and most analog synths have an ADSR function. *Attack* refers to how quickly the sound reaches its maximum level after a note is played. A piano has a very fast attack: the moment you hit the keys, the piano produces sound at its maximum levels. On the other hand, with something such as a horn, you can have a slow build-up of volume (like a swell) until the note hits its high point. This is a very slow attack. On a synth, when you program a fast attack, the note strikes its high level as the key is depressed. If a slow attack is programmed, the sound may take a few seconds to build up to its maximum strength. As such, attack determines how fast a note gets "turned on," like a dimmer switch on a lamp that can make the light either get brighter slowly or as bright as possible.

Decay is an indication of how fast the sound goes from its maximum attack level down to its sustain level. *Sustain* refers to how long the note holds over time. Shortening this function gives you choppier sounds like percussion (which have very little sustain), while lengthening it carries the tone out for varying lengths of time.

Normally, sustain will cause the sound to fade out into nothingness after a few seconds. However, since synths use keys to activate sounds, releasing those keys is given a function as well, known as *release.* Setting the release function will determine if the sustain drops off quickly after fingers are taken off the keys, like on a regular piano, or if the sound continues to sustain over a predetermined period of time. Look at it in the context of a real piano. If you hit a note with your finger, and leave it depressed, the note will sustain until the strings inside the piano stop vibrating. If you take your finger off the key, the sound immediately stops as the strings are damped. This sudden cessation of sound is due to the speed of the release of the finger. On a synth, though, the amount of time left in the sustain after taking your finger off the key may be programmed. So instead of immediately stopping the sound, the synth still may give it another second or two or three of sustain, or it may stop it completely. On synths, unlike other instruments, the release is variable.

All of this is pretty easy to see on a graph, much like our waveform graphs. Figure 5–3 gives you a good idea of how ADSR works over time. Essentially, all an envelope generator does is assign specific values of each point in the ADSR envelope to the sound being produced. It does this by determining how fast or how slow the voltage rises from zero to its maximum point and then back to zero again. Once this is determined—by the

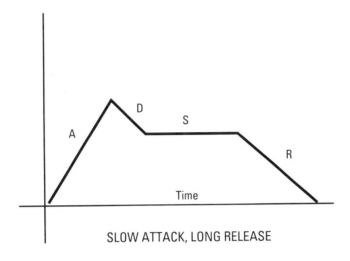

SLOW ATTACK, LONG RELEASE

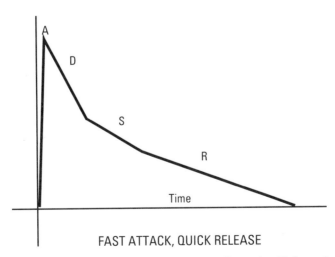

FAST ATTACK, QUICK RELEASE

Figure 5–3. **ADSR (Attack, Delay, Sustain, Release) points on a sound envelope.**

user's setting of controls—the envelope generator produces a signal in the desired shape of the ADSR which it sends to the voltage devices. The voltage devices then apply this shape, called an envelope, to the sound they are creating. Then the sounds start, sustain, and stop according to the user's wishes.

LIMITATIONS OF EARLY SYNTHESIZERS

No true analog synth is complete without an input device. Although different people had different ideas on input—everything from heat to magnets—keyboards became the accepted method for selecting the notes from the VCO. Keyboards worked well because they had very definite ON and OFF points. Depressed down was ON, let up was OFF. Very, very easy to understand, and just as easy to operate. But as far as synths in the early days went, that was the *only* easy part.

In order to control the VCO, a key was pressed. Nothing more, nothing less. But to affect the workings of the other parts of the synthesizer, electrical signals had to be manually directed to perform their tasks. In those early days, there was no simple turning of one knob, or pushing of one button. Shaping a sound involved plugging dozens and dozens of wires into different plugs on a synthesizer to get VCOs, VCAs, and ADSR functions to behave in the proper manner. This part of the synth, the workings away from the keyboard, looked exactly like an old-time telephone operator's station. You may have seen them in museums or reruns of *The Andy Griffith Show:* huge wall-sized boards with hundreds of tiny input holes (each about the size of a standard quarter-inch phone jack) and dangling wires running from hole to hole. Anytime the operator wanted to put a call through, She would say "One moment, puh-leee-yuz," and then switch one end of a cable from this hole to that hole. This way, calls were routed from the caller to the proper location.

Early synths were a lot like that. When a synth player wanted to change the sound of a tone, he or she had to route the sound through different parts of the control board. Every change, like every phone call, required re-routing the cables to a new position. And just as with the early telephone operators, who would patch a caller through by inserting cables into the proper holes, the process of creating different sounds resulted from assigning cables to new positions, or patching them into place. It is from this procedure that we get the term *patch* for a particular configuration that creates a sound. Even in this new-and-improved digital age, we still refer to individual sounds as *patches,* though the process we use today is not even remotely like the one just described, and doesn't involve patch cables. Good thing, too, because in modern society, where we want everything yesterday, this type of synth was almost hopelessly slow.

Yet patching wasn't the worst drawback of the first synths. The worst part of these synths was the fact that they were completely monophonic. This means they could only play one note at a time. *Only* one. If you placed two fingers on the keyboard at the same time, one would cancel out while the other played on. No two-handed chords, no holding of sustained notes on the left hand with trills on the right. One note, and one note only, at a time. This was because the oscillators could only handle one input at a time from the keyboard section of the synth. It was just too much to expect—in time, money, and size—to have a synth play more than one note.

People like Isao Tomita, Walter (now Wendy) Carlos, Keith Emerson, and Rick Wakeman thus were forced to put layer upon layer of individual notes on top of each other when recording using this wonderful instrument known as a synthesizer. Patch changes or wiring up individual sounds could also take up to several minutes, and this added to the time-consuming process. Clearly, synths in the late 1960s and early 1970s were not for the faint of heart.

Things changed slowly, but they did change. Small versions of these monstrous patch-crazed machines began to hit the consumer market around 1973, marketed by companies like Moog and ARP. These manufacturers replaced the enormous array of patches, switches, and knobs with sliders (which are called faders when used as volume controls), knobs, and buttons, and limited the amount of gymnastics a musician had to perform in order to get a decent sound. (I have seen novices stand in front of an ARP 2600 for over half an hour and still not get it to produce a *single* sound, let alone any melodies.) Machines like the Mini-Moog and ARP Odyssey brought the world of high-technology synthesis—as well as mandatory one-note playing—to the music world for only a few thousand dollars. While that was quite a bit of money in those days, many musicians immediately fell prostrate in front of these machines as if they were the saviors of modern music. And it was quite amazing what these musicians could do with one note at a time, especially when it came to soloing. For instance, listen to "Baba O'Riley" on the *Who's Next* album.

Pete Townshend was one of the first rock musicians to see the potential of synths. Or listen to Keith Emerson's solo at the end of ELP's "Lucky Man." These are good examples of the early commercial use of the monophonic synthesizer.

POLYPHONIC SYNTHESIS

Hurdles don't last long in the face of technology, and monophonic synths were no exception. The next natural step was to increase the number of keys that could be activated at any one time—in effect, to create polyphony.

Most acoustic instruments are polyphonic to some degree, with the obvious exception of percussion instruments, certain horns, and wood-winds. This latter category is limited primarily to single-note forms of playing. But guitars, pianos, banjos, organs, and most other instruments are capable of producing more than one sound at any given moment. If you press all ten fingers on a piano keyboard, you get ten different notes; if you strum all six open strings on a guitar, you get six different notes. These are examples of polyphony—creating more than one note sound at the same time.

Actually, the best example of a monophonic instrument is your voice. At any one time, you can only produce a specific note. You can create lots of different notes with your voice, but they have to follow one after the other. No two can ever be sounded at once.

This was the dilemma facing monophonic synthesizers. All those keys just sitting there, arranged in standard fashion, and only one at a time could be used.

In 1975, Oberheim introduced the Modular-4, a polyphonic synthe-sizer. Followed by the Moog Mini-Moog and the Sequential Circuits Prophet-5, these synths could accept up to eight notes *simultaneously.* If you added more fingers (after all, there *are* normally ten fingers on two hands, not just eight), the synth would start removing previous notes in one of two ways: it would either take the very first notes that were depressed and reassign them to the new notes (such as when adding a Sus4 to a chord), or it would eliminate them by position on the keyboard (low notes get sacrificed for new higher notes, or vice versa). Whatever the method, it sure beat one-note-at-a-time polyphony, and who uses ten fingers at one time *all* the time anyway? Synths for use in the real world were born.

As technology shrunk more and more of the components used in electronic equipment down to near-microscopic sizes, synth manufacturers found that they could start offering more features and more control in synths geared for musicians who made less than $100,000 a year. Part of this innovation was the complete conversion of control to push buttons, sliders, and an occasional knob. Now selection of sound types (notably on instruments by Roland) was a question of real-time button and slider pushing. Sounds could be changed on the fly (in real-time) to produce bizarre effects, as a single sound went from a cello-like tone to a gurgling cacophony of strange underworld noises. And it could be done while playing chords! By this time, patching chords had become just a memory, and fingertip control was *in*.

The widespread use of microprocessors in computers in the late 1970s led to their eventual use in everything from stereos to microwaves to synthesizers. As we've seen in other chapters, microprocessors are completely digital in nature, and therefore allow for more control by the user than analog systems. The first natural merging of digital microprocessors with analog synths resulted in a variety of digitally controlled analog synths in the late 1970s and early 1980s. Among the primary manufacturers of these synths were Oberheim, Sequential Circuits, Roland, Korg, and Yamaha. These machines usually started with a *digitally* controlled oscillator (DCO). Produced by a microprocessor, the frequencies generated by these oscillators were a lot more stable and, thus, easier to control. In fact, they could be selected with the push of a button (or combination of buttons) for immediate use of any desired waveform. The rest of the synth setup remained essentially the same, with VCFs, VCAs, and envelope generators making up the analog portion of the system, with the proper sliders and switches.

Most of the music industry switched to the digitally controlled analog synths from 1979 to 1983 because of their simplicity and multiple range of features, not to mention that they required less setup and programming time—thanks to the microprocessor. However, the whole ballgame changed forever in 1983, when *completely* digital synthesis replaced analog methodology once and for all.

DIGITAL SYNTHESIS

Since the early 1970s, John Chowning, a Stanford University professor, had been experimenting with the digital production and control of frequency modulation (FM). Frequency modulation relates to the changing of a specific waveform's frequency over time, but its benefit to musicians lies in the *way* frequency modulation creates interesting harmonic frequencies that change slightly over time. This change gives sound a fuller and richer quality, because the changing harmonics are often slightly detuned as they evolve. Acoustic instruments produce this effect naturally, but it was difficult to control with analog synths because of the complexity of the evolving waveforms.

Yamaha DX-7

Chowning perfected a technique of producing FM waveforms using computer-controlled processes. The result were sounds which had much more of the natural complexity and fullness of "real" sounds. This technique ended up going from the labs at Stanford to the inside of the Yamaha DX-7, the first all-digital commercial synthesizer. With the DX-7, sounds were stored digitally in the synth's internal memory and sound cartridges as combinations of FM sounds (which Yamaha called operators). Each of these sounds could be retrieved from inside the machine with the mere press of a button. No oscillators, filters, amplifiers, or envelope generators to adjust and monkey with—just a complete sound, set and ready to go. (See Fig. 5–4.)

Before we go any further, two points need to be made about digital synthesizers. The first is that with the introduction of the DX-7, synthesizers became as much computers as they were sound-producing machines. Microprocessing, memory, and all-digital functions are part and parcel of computers, and now they are part and parcel of synths. Memory is the most important function of these synths, and in most cases, external memory devices like cartridges and memory cards allow the musician to add more sounds to his or her arsenal. This ability to insert and remove whole banks of sounds with a simple plastic cartridge/card/disk is what takes the capabilities of digital synths light years away from the limitations of analog synths.

Secondly, even though these sounds were called up from the synth's memory with the push of a button, the experienced user could actually tweak certain parts of the sounds by entering the programming mode of the synth. While a majority of the people using synths never even activate this function of digital synths and just use the sounds as they are stored,

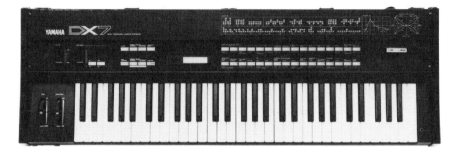

Figure 5-4. Yamaha DX7 FM digital synthesizer.

the feature is there for those who wish to customize sounds. As such, digital synths still retain some of the flexibility originally found on analog synths in the way of programming.

More than 100,000 units of the DX-7 were sold in its first three years, making it the most popular synth ever produced up until that time. The fact that it had removed any *necessary* programming so that the musician could get on with the function of playing sounds was the single most important development in bringing synths to the mass market.

Soon, every recording seemed to have a DX-7 on it, and DX-7 sounds became readily recognizable to anyone familiar with the instrument. Almost overnight, a host of other variations on FM synthesis in general, and digital synthesis in particular, appeared from a number of manufacturers, notably digital phase distortion by Casio (a technology and product which were actually developed at the same time as the DX-7). At the same time, the analog synth began to gather dust as it lost its appeal and, by 1987, was almost completely relegated to use as an instrument for producing "weird" sounds.

The DX-7 and other Yamaha FM-based equipment such as drum machines dominated the marketplace from 1983 until 1987. When you think about it, four years for any technology to dominate any market in this day and age is pretty phenomenal, given that the average implementation of a new technology and new equipment runs only about 18 to 24 months. This means that newer, better stuff is usually only two years away, *max.* Fortunately, MIDI keeps any of this from being obsolete (see MIDI chapter), but today's musician is faced with a bewildering array of choices every one-and-a-half to two years, which can be tough on the bank account. Unfortunately, there is nothing that can be done about this. You have to make the best decisions at the time and then plan for the next time you can afford to invest in new technology. (From personal experience, a three-year cycle of investment in new equipment/technology seems to work pretty well.)

Roland D-50

In 1987, the second major digital-synth bombshell was dropped on the commercial music market. Roland introduced its D-50, a synth based on *linear arithmetic* techniques. Although trying to understand "LA synthesis" (as it is called) can make you feel as if bees are living inside your head, I'll give you a basic description in just a few sentences.

Linear arithmetic is a type of arithmetic used for certain types of computer calculations. In the D-50 (and other products in Roland's LA-based series), a number of sound pieces, called partials, are stored in memory. Combining any two partials creates a tone, and combining any two tones produces a complete patch. Partials were created by the manufacturer from either actual samples or digitally synthesized sounds. Each of the partials contains functions which allow for tweaking by the user (filters, amplifiers, envelope generators, etc.) in a programming mode. And the D-50 has some pretty deep levels of programming that make pure computer programming look like child's play.

But Roland combined these partials into some incredibly lifelike patches. Like the DX-7, the D-50 required no programming ability to get some great sounds out of the synth. Roland also took great pains to include some of the stranger "space-drool" sounds normally found on analog synths as part of the factory sounds. One patch in particular, "Digital

Figure 5–5.   Roland D-50 digital synthesizer.

Native Dance," found its way unmodified onto albums by the Cars, Rick Springfield, and David Lee Roth within months of the D-50's introduction. (See Fig. 5–5.)

The D-50 also came with an extensive set of digital effects that could be added to the patches—from the synth itself! This meant that the musician could assign different levels of reverb or equalization to the patches before they were even played, and then have those effects be a part of the sound. In many cases, this eliminated the need for an outside effects module. Why run the D-50 through a digital reverb unit when it had one *internally?*

With all of these features, the D-50 supplanted the DX-7 as *the* synth of the late 1980s. Even today, it is the standard for all commercial synths that aren't entirely sample-based. The full range of effects, plus the wide variety of lifelike sounds combined with not-so-lifelike sounds, provides the D-50 with enough features to cater to almost any musician's needs. While the programming environment is intricate, it is as rich as any synth technician might hope to find. The major drawback—I daresay, problem —with the D-50, is the fact that it is not *multi-timbral.* We'll look at this term and its importance to modern synth playing in a moment.

Korg M1

Currently, Korg's M1 synthesizer is a contender for the "next big synth for the masses" award. Utilizing a technology that Korg calls AI (advanced integrated) synthesis, the machine features realistic sound patches, is multi-timbral (which the D-50 is not), and has a small on-board sequencer. While the M1 is still a relatively new entry in the field, the fact that it is multi-timbral gives it an advantage over its competition.

Other Digital Synths

A number of other digital synths are worth looking at while we're in this chapter. Although not geared exclusively to the commercial market, they set the "Rolls Royce" standards for digital synthesis, and offer the professional musician—with the right amount of money—everything he or she might want in a complete musical setup.

Two of these synths really belong in the same category—an exclusive category which borders on the unaffordable. They are the PPG Fairlight, and the New England Digital Synclavier.

It's hard to describe these pieces of machinery simply as synths, be-cause they are actually complete music workstations (Fig. 5–6). In addition to a keyboard, built-in sampler, built-in computer and monitor, built-in editing features, built-in synthesis techniques, and a host of other features; these systems also provide options for digital recording direct-to-disk.

All of this is built into a complete workstation about the size of a spinet piano. It's really more like sitting down to a true computer than to a synthesizer. However, all of these features and functions come with two formidable, and perhaps fearsome, barriers to entry: a learning curve of weeks, months, and even years, and a starting price tag of over $100,000. For that much money, I would expect it to get up and cook me breakfast in the morning, as well as compute my taxes, in addition to helping me create, perform, and record my music.

Both of these products have features which make them different

Figure 5–6.   New England Digital Synclavier work station.

from each other, but they essentially compete exclusively against each other for the very highest dollars in the market. Both, however, have been around for much of the last decade, and have functions that are a bit outdated. Critics decry them as dinosaurs, while some of the few that own them find that there is absolutely no substitute for them in terms of a complete electronic music environment.

Times they are a-changing, though. As of this writing, reports are that Fairlight has closed its doors and is no longer producing its product. And in my opinion, though the Synclavier has everything one might ever need all combined into one product, the same type of system can be created equally as well—and perhaps better—by building a music system composed of different components from different manufacturers, for *thousands* of dollars less. This will have an impact on the Synclavier's popularity over the long term. People still buy Rolls Royces, though, so you never really can tell.

One other synth worth mentioning is the Kurzweil. Raymond Kurzweil is a whiz at electronic ingenuity, and in addition to creating Kurzweil Music Systems, he invented a machine that "reads" books to the blind, and a computer device that recognizes human voices and allows computers to be controlled by voice instead of by a keyboard. Very fond of self-promotion, Kurzweil has never been shy about billing his products as the best on the market. The Kurzweil 250 Synthesizer may or may not be an exception to his claims, except that its high price tag keeps it from addressing the mass market the way that Roland and Yamaha do (Fig. 5–7).

Known simply as "the Kurzweil" throughout the industry, this synth uses techniques from an extremely advanced area of high technology called artificial intelligence (AI) to produce its remarkably accurate sounds. AI is the field of computer science that attempts to emulate human behavior, specifically thinking, reasoning, and understanding, in computers—in short, give computers some semblance of intelligence. Kurzweil (the person) has long been a proponent of AI technologies, and employs them in the Kurzweil 250 (which I'll call the K250 from here on in). AI is one of the most incredibly complex areas of computer research, so any attempt to define its applications here would be just like getting near the iceberg, not even scraping the tip of it. (There is a discussion of what AI may achieve in the musical future in Chapter Twelve). The AI used in the K250 *anticipates* what the patch should actually sound like, and blends together a number of samples, waveforms, and digitally produced data to produce a complex, but

Figure 5–7.   Kurzweil K250 digital synthesizer.

very realistic, sound. The K250 also features a sampling option, which brings us to another class of synths discussed next: the sampling keyboard.

The K250 performs especially well in duplicating the sound of real acoustic pianos, especially grand pianos. Most other synths, regardless of technique, have fallen short of providing the market with a truly accurate grand piano sound. The K250's almost flawless replication of a grand piano sound brought it to immediate fame, if not fortune. Priced originally at $15,000, this was not the kind of synth you saved up for six months to buy. At that kind of price level, only studios and professional musicians could afford to own and cherish the Kurzweil.

All of the above manufacturers (except for PPG and New England Digital) have various models of their famous keyboards available across the price spectrum, and also as sound module components—meaning they are available as rack-mounted modules without keyboards attached. Thus, you can buy a K250 or a D-50 in a box, and get those sounds by using another keyboard synth, or even a guitar and wind synth. The examples above are not intended to give you the impression that these manufacturers' product lines are limited to their flagship products; quite the contrary. There are all kinds of options and versions available (at both higher and lower prices) which make access to most of these synth technologies "doable," if not always reasonable. You'll be forced to agonize over whether to buy now, or whether to wait until that "unannounced" upgrade version is available in six months, and it will probably drive you crazy. But this is what keeps the synth manufacturers in business, and its no different than car manufacturers. Models improve, get extra features, and replace old models. But you can't wait forever. If you do, you'll never get a new synth, or a new car. High-tech buying fear is a normal condition; it's as inescapable as paying taxes. And though you can put off taxes for as long as possible, if you do the same with electronic instruments, you'll miss the boat. Which means you'll miss the trip, and it's one of the best around for musicians.

Sampling Keyboards

In 1985, Ensoniq, a synth manufacturer made up of ex-Commodore computer personnel, introduced the Mirage, the first truly affordable sampling keyboard. Sampling keyboards had been available for a while (mostly as parts of machines like the Synclavier), but only at prices equal to the cost of the average Ferrari or the average home in Seattle. Sampling keyboards are sampling modules that have built-in keyboards, much like normal synths. (See Fig. 5–8.) The sound source is a disk-drive sampler, as opposed to internally synthesized sounds. Without the sampling disk, the keyboard produces no sound of its own. The Mirage combined the features of a stand-alone sampler with a controller keyboard in one complete unit, which worked out nicely for musicians who only wanted to use samples and not monkey around with additional forms of synthesis (like hooking up a D-50 to an E-max sampler).

Figure 5–8.   Ensoniq Mirage-DSK sampling keyboard.

These keyboards now proliferate from most of the major manufacturers, and many have a built-in sequencing option for storing songs (see Chapter Eight for an in-depth discussion of sequencing). This gives rise to a whole *other* class of synths known as sequencing keyboards, which provide for internal sequencing and storage of songs without having to resort to outside devices or software.

DIGITAL CAPABILITY

Now that we've talked about where digital synths came from and how they work, it's time to look at some of the features that they offer that were never even considered in the realm of analog synths.

MIDI

MIDI and digital synths go together like a hand and a glove, pancakes and maple syrup, Frick and Frack, Mickey and Minnie, and every other tired cliché that you can think of. Without digital synths, there would be no MIDI. On the other hand, MIDI helps the musician exploit the full potential of a digital synth. Features like program changing and controllers can best be manipulated through MIDI. For a full description of how, consult Chapter Four.

Multi-Timbral Synths versus Voices

Voices are the number of sounds that a digital synth can activate at one time. Even though this sounds simple, it is one of the most confusing aspects of using a digital synth. People are forever confusing voices with polyphony, so pay close attention and learn the difference in the following paragraph. The professional embarrassment you save may be your own.

We talked earlier about the difference between monophonic and polyphonic synthesizers. Monophonic synths only make sound for one note at a time. Polyphonic synths can play multiple notes simultaneously. At one time, people referred to this difference as being the number of *voices* that a synth had. A monophonic machine only had one voice, a polyphonic device was a multi-voice synth.

At that time, though, both mono- and polyphonic synths could play only one sound (patch) at a time. This meant that the sound coming out of every note was the same *sound*. Not the same note, the same sound. If eight keys were depressed while using a flute patch, all eight notes gave forth their note values with the sound of a flute. This should make sense; you select a patch, and every key pressed sounds like the patch. Seems pretty normal, doesn't it? (See Fig. 5–9.)

Not so fast. With the advent of digital technology, certain synths had the capability of allowing more than one sound to be used *at a time.* Here's where it gets confusing. If you wanted your left hand to sound like a cello, and your right hand to sound like a flute, you could program each section of the keyboard to address a certain patch. Thus, everything below middle C would sound like a cello, and everything above middle C would sound like a flute (Fig. 5–10). This provided a whole new level of flexibility for the keyboard player.

In some cases, the keyboard could be divided up as many as eight different ways, allowing for a whole symphony section to be resident on the keyboard at once. Synths that have this function are known as *multi-timbral* synths. They have access to two or more sounds simultaneously. But with flagrant disregard for the terminology of earlier years, people started calling these *multi-voice* synthesizers. A keyboard that could access

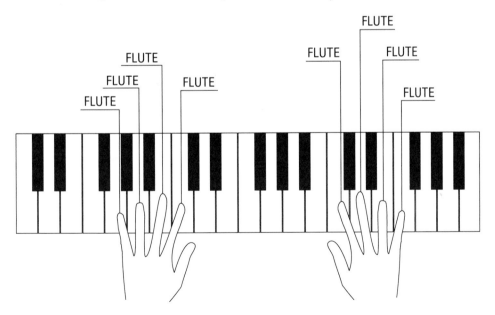

Figure 5–9. Polyphonic non-multi-timbral synthesizer.

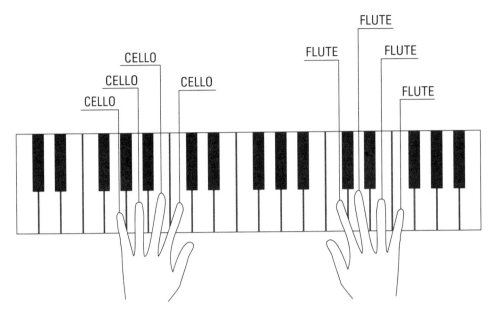

Figure 5–10.   Keyboard split into two voices.

eight sounds at a time became known as an *eight-voice* synth (Fig. 5–11). In this context, multi-timbral and multi-voice mean the same thing; they do *not* refer to the number of notes that can be played at one time.

Let me be a bit more specific. No matter how you program the D-50, you are only going to get one *patch* out of the instrument at a time (techno-head purists will argue that you can split partials into upper and lower keyboard positions, but that's not what I'm talking about here). You put ten fingers down on the D-50 keyboard at once, you're going to get ten notes all with the *same* sound, whether it's strings, electronic pianos, steel drums, or oboes. This is because it is *not* multi-timbral. Conversely, if you use an Ensoniq ESQ synth, which *is* multi-timbral, you could put *ten* fingers down and have them activate *eight* different sounds, or voices. Which fingers sounded which patches would be determined by the way you assigned the patches to the parts of the keyboard. In some cases, you could assign a patch to just a single key, so that only when that key was depressed would that sound be produced.

Being multi-timbral extends to MIDI applications as well. If you're controlling your synth with a guitar controller, a non-multi-timbral synth will assign the same voice to all six strings (Fig. 5–12). If you're using the

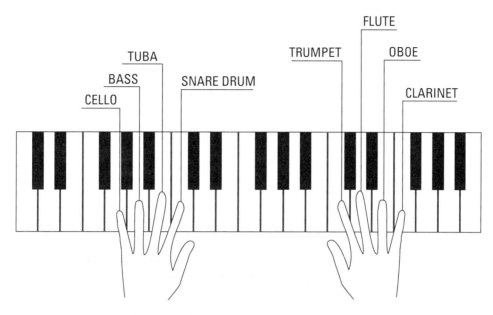

Figure 5–11. Multi-timbral synth with eight voices assigned to individual keys.

guitar controller with a multi-timbral synth, then each string can be assigned its own sound. This means that as you strum you could theoretically be activating a violin, a harp, a flute, a snare drum, a cello, and a bass simultaneously (Fig. 5–13).

If you are still with me, we have almost captured the hill. Regardless of how many sound patches you've assigned to your multi-timbral keyboard, the number of available polyphonic notes *doesn't* increase. If your synth can only handle ten notes at a time, that's all you get, period. Each patch doesn't get ten notes—the entire keyboard does. This fact remains unchanged despite the ability to add more sounds in the multi-timbral mode. This gets skewed a little in the MIDI MONO mode, but that only occurs during MIDI operation (again, consult Chapter Four for specifics).

In summary: When we say "voices" in reference to digital synths, we are talking about whether or not a synth has multi-timbral capability. A one-voice synth is not multi-timbral, while an eight-voice synth *is* multi-timbral. "Eight-voice synth" used to mean you could sound eight *notes* at once (originally applied to analog synths); but the term now refers to the ability to activate eight *sounds* at once (applied to multi-timbral digital synths).

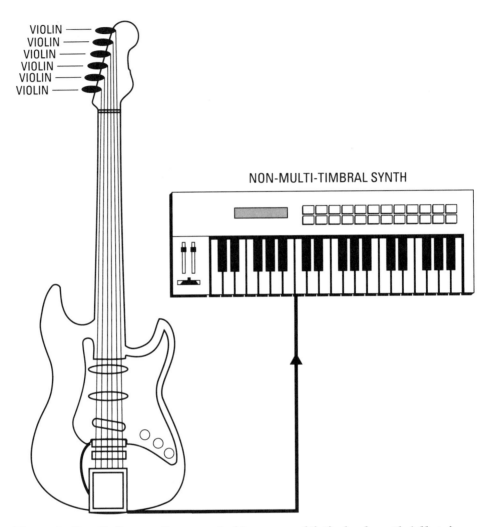

Figure 5–12. Guitar synth connected to non-multi-timbral synth (all strings have the same voice).

Memory

As stressed earlier, the ability to keep patches in memory is what really makes digital synths a luxury over analog synths. With analog synths, each time you wanted a new sound, you had to build or create it from the ground up. With digital synths, these patches are stored either internally

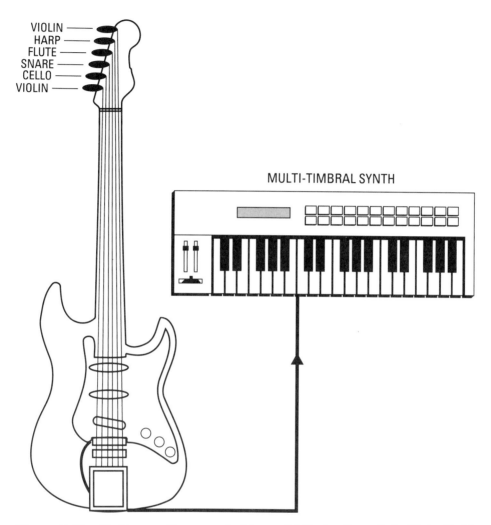

VIOLIN ——
HARP ——
FLUTE ——
SNARE ——
CELLO ——
VIOLIN ——

MULTI-TIMBRAL SYNTH

Figure 5–13. **Guitar synth connected to multi-timbral synth (with individual string assignments).**

and/or on a removable memory medium like a cartridge or disk. Even when the synth is turned off, the patches stay in memory exactly as they were before it was shut down.

Since these patches are all in memory, they can be arranged in specific ways to meet your needs, much as you would arrange books by a certain category. Moving the sounds does not alter them, but it makes calling them up for use in a particular order especially easy. The process of doing this is usually accomplished with the aid of specific types of software known as "librarians." Librarians are often grouped together with another type of software called "editors" which provide a much more convenient method of changing sound parameters with the use of a personal computer. It's hard to adjust waveforms looking at those little tiny display panels on the front of a synth, and software editors make all the difference in the world. Such manipulation can be stored in memory, either as a completely new patch (which you name) or as a permanent change to the original patch. This flexibility in memory, as well as the removable and portable memory medium of cartridges and the like, means that your changes and modifications to patches can be made at a convenient time for you, and don't have to be made during a live performance or a recording session. Unlike days of old, digital technology allows you to prepare for your gigs or recording dates well in advance of the actual event, saving you plenty of time, money, premature hair loss, ulcers, and stress-induced migraines.

THE USE OF SYNTHESIZERS

All of this has affected how synths are actually *used*. Originally, synthesizers allowed musicians to create and use sounds no one had ever heard before. Part of the appeal of early Emerson, Lake & Palmer, or Wendy Carlos recordings was the musical use of strange electronic sounds in compositions and performance. The weird pitch bends, the unusual timbres, and completely alien sounds gave synths a unique place in the music of the late 1960s and early 1970s.

Over time, the musicians using synths found that they could control them enough to make them sound *somewhat* similar to other types of instruments, notably string and horn sections. This began to take hold in bands that did not employ string or horn players. Even though these sounds had an electronic timbre (described as a "cold sizzle"), they were passable—or perhaps recognizable—as attempts to emulate normal acoustic instruments.

The emphasis on the synthesizer as a unique, strange-sounding instrument with its own characteristics is largely gone now. Certainly some incredible and unearthly sounds still come out of synths, but for the large part, synth players want their instruments to sound "real." The more accurate sounding the grand-piano patch, the trumpet patch, the cello patch, or the pumpkin patch, the more desirable the synth is apt to be. Hence, the overwhelming popularity of digital synths, and the near-extinction of analog synths.

But this has brought about a change in the way synth players have to play. Using these sounds in a realistic and recognizable manner requires a bit of modification on the part of the synth player. When emulating a saxophone player, a standard keyboard block triad isn't going to sound like a saxophone—no matter what. This is because sax players do not use block triads in their playing. Thus, a synth player trying to get that true sax sound must think and play as if he were actually using a sax; single note runs, trills, arpeggios, and so on. (Of course, there will always be performers who use such methods as part of artistic shock value.) But the person who truly wishes to emulate another type of musician with a particular patch sound must be willing to give up playing the controller as its own instrument.

For instance, a keyboard player on a synth can't play hammer-handed and expect to sound like a concert cellist, and a guitarist with a controller can't expect to strum away and sound like a practiced flautist. The style of playing must be modified to match the sound of the patch. Only in this way can synth players hope to accomplish the illusion of playing another instrument.

Samplers are the best indication of this desire to recreate truly accurate sounds. But the more precise the sound emulation, the less control we tend to have over it. With older synths, every single variable of the machine and its sounds was determined by the player. In fact, the synth created *no* sounds unless the player performed a certain amount of programming. Now, however, sounds tend to be preprogrammed with only a certain amount of immediate modification available to the user. Today's digital synths have turned synthesists from programmers back into performers, but have also taught them to be keenly aware of how synthesized sounds must behave in order to simulate reality.

WHAT'S NEXT?

Now that we've had a look at digital synthesizers, we'll look at the other machines of music that the digital revolution has brought upon us, and how they can be used either independently or in conjunction with synths to create and enhance your musical pursuits. As this chapter comes to a close, and as you look back on all of these classes and types and variations of the venerable synthesizer, your reaction to all of this synth technology may be: "Where will it all end?"

Fortunately, it won't. As mentioned in the introduction, even though many of these types and classes overlap (like sampling keyboards with sequencing capabilities), newer and more powerful keyboards with newer and more exciting features will continue to appear on the horizon. They will always come down in price after a period of time (thanks to the economics of supply and demand), providing features and functions to musicians that even five years ago would have been thought impossible, let alone affordable. This means that at some point, just about every technology is within reach of every musician. That's a pretty good deal.

It's a good thing that all this development won't end. The ultimate winner in the battle to create new machines from new technology is the musician.

6

Drums, Guitars, and Winds

he terms "music" and "technology" traditionally conjure up visions of synthesizers, from the early hulking monsters replete with knobs and patch cables to today's ultra-sleek, jet-black digital keyboards. Since keyboards were the first musical instruments to get the high-tech treatment, this is only natural. But in the past few years, other instruments, other devices, and other types of musicians have stormed the temple of technology, claiming computerization and technological advancements in the name of percussion, stringed instruments, wind instruments, and even the human voice.

No longer are keyboard players the sole proprietors of dazzling technology. Almost every other instrument type has its own modern machine icons which allow musicians to safely enter the digital age. This chapter looks at the instruments and devices—the machines—which are making technology a tool of every musician.

DRUM MACHINES

The most prevalent example of technology's stranglehold on music is the drum machine. Every form of music from reggae to rock and country to dance music has liberally employed the drum machine. As an example, dance music's primary instrument is the drum machine—everything else is secondary, and probably gets in the way of the resounding crashes of the percussion.

Even bands that traditionally use human drummers have employed drum machines both live and in the studio for certain effects or unusual rhythms and patterns. But before any of you bemoan the death of the human drummer in modern music, remember one crucial factor: the best person to program and operate a drum machine is a *drummer.* The patterns involved in even a simple four-beat drum piece are enough to confuse almost everyone who is not an experienced drummer. Sure, you can use the factory programs, and try to get by with those, but it's like kissing your sister: it may have the same basis as the real thing, but it's not very exciting and it doesn't get you very far.

Drum machine is a catch-all term used to describe an electronic instrument that is either activated by hitting it (like a drum) or that produces various types of percussion sounds. Actually, the former example is more specifically a drum trigger or electronic drum/pad, but for the sake of categorization, it gets lumped in with drum machines. We'll explore both of these types of instruments and find out what makes them click (pun *definitely* intended).

The History

Rhythm machines have been around for years as part of large performance organs and even home organ systems. A single click of a button, or flick of a switch, and the organ player could activate some preprogrammed (which also meant unchangeable) rhythms such as swing, Bossa Nova, waltz, samba, rock 4-beat, and a variety of other patterns. There is still some affinity in the musical community between keyboard synths and drum machines, almost as if manufacturers look at them as being two peas in a pod.

The late 1970s ushered in the first programmable drum machines, presented by Oberheim and Linn Drum. These bulky creatures, about the size of small suitcases, were the first devices that gave rhythm players an alternative to carting around two dozen pieces of percussion from stage to stage, studio to studio, or practice place to practice place. As with the digital synth, the introduction of microtechnology finally produced a size- and cost-efficient alternative to massive drum setups. Actually, cost was way out of sight at first, but has since come into line with the average musician's pocketbook, like most other technological developments. Almost all the early versions of drum machines were used in studios.

The advantages to using these machines in studios were enormous. A basic track could be laid down very quickly without having to set up a drum kit with each of its corresponding mikes, and without having to have an area the size of a small airplane hangar to set up in. Depending on the disposition of the drummer, *he* didn't even have to be there to lay down simple guide drums.

Especially worthwhile was the fact that these machines could be plugged directly into the recording console without any amplification. As anyone who has ever had to sit in the same practice room or recording booth with a drummer for an extended period of time knows, repeated takes can often lead to temporary deafness, irritability, crankiness, and partial insanity—and this is just on the part of the listener. The effect it has on drummers is truly horrible to behold. Drum machines thus eliminated some of the most basic logistics of setting up percussion in a studio setting.

At this time, from the mid-1970s on, drum manufacturers and professional drummers began to take a more active role in their craft. Tunable drums, cylindrical drums, flange-shaped drums, Octobans, and Roto-Toms soon became components of the percussionist's arsenal, which heretofore had been limited to a basic trap kit involving four drums, a cymbal or two, and a hi-hat. With this expansion into the further realms of drumming and the advent of unusual electronic components, drummers and manufacturers only needed one more catalyst to push them into the world of electronic drums. They got it with the arrival of disco.

Whatever your feelings about disco (I can't print mine, since I'm sure to offend those with a more delicate sensibility), its incessantly repetitious drum beat paved the way for both the common use of drum machines and for the practical use of electronic drums. Using drum machines that could repeat patterns over and over and over eliminated the need for a studio drummer. This may or may not have worked against drummers, since many of them refused to sit for five to eight minutes repeating the exact same four-beat pattern. As live bands were forced to play disco in clubs, drummers also found that they needed to create other unusual percussive sounds to augment the tedium of the disco beat. What emerged was a class of drum pad that was shaped like a small, flat tom-tom, but instead of generating any sound of its own, these drums produced percussive synthesized sounds. At first this was done by striking the pads and activating the pressure-sensitive electronics underneath a rubber head. The electronics were wired to a small sound module which produced weird little "byoo-byoo-byoos," "ee-ee-ees," and "do-do-dos" in a manner very reminiscent of early analog synths. But they served as interesting sounds for fills or an occasional roll, so they made their way into the market and onto record.

As disco gave way to the more listenable techno-pop, drummers found the need to be able to create even more unusual percussion sounds that were not then available on keyboard synthesizers. A lot of this had to do with the speed at which a drummer could activate a series of sounds, which was—and is—faster than most keyboard players. The nature of percussive attack (no rising attack wave and minimal sustain) also added an intriguing feature to the possibilities of allowing drummers control over greater sound varieties.

Two types of electronic drum implementation came into vogue—an actual electronic setup that was made to look, feel, and act like a standard drum kit, and a component with a flat surface that was divided into separate pads in order to simulate different drums. Simmons Drums pioneered the use of the "electronic drumkit" while synth manufacturers like Roland developed the flat-pad based Octapad. Each of these systems allowed the drummer to activate different sounds from different drums, and still have control over the individual characteristics of each sound. The problem that remained, however, was that all of these drums sounded like synthesized drums. While that was certainly a plus for unusual percussion effects, it didn't help the musician who wanted true drum sounds out of his electronic drums. (Recall that this was the original bane of synth players who wanted their Moogs to sound like Steinways.)

In the mid-1980s, MIDI crept into the drummer's realm, and now those weird-sounding devices could hook up to synths, samplers, and other assorted sound modules. Not only did the drums access more realistic drum sounds, but they could also access and activate other "musical" sounds such as harpsichord patches, weird alien-sounding patches, symphonic string patches, and human voice samples. This meant that both the live and studio drummer could add sounds on top of a roll or triple flim-flam, while still getting drum sounds out of the instrument. Thus, in live performance, the drummer could take over many of the simpler keyboard duties, especially when sound effects or single instrument bursts were required.

The Workings

A drum machine works essentially the same way as a digital synth, and in some cases a sampler, does. It has onboard sounds that correspond to a specific button or key, and rarely can the user alter the sound of the individual drums as they are programmed at the factory. This is because the drum sounds are "burned in" to the machine's microprocessor memory, so that each time a particular button is pressed, the same sound—without variation—is always retrieved from memory. This "burning in" is really just a way to make sure that the sounds are forever in memory and can't be screwed up by the user. Some models actually allow you to modify the sounds through some basic programming, but this is really more the exception than the rule. This is all done in the computer's ROM, or "Read Only Memory," which is just what it sounds like—a memory that only lets you read information from it without being able to alter the data. ROMs are sort of like CDs or record albums; once you've bought them, they never change. You can't alter the way the information is stored on an album or CD. Contrast that with a cassette tape, which can be re-recorded, played over, and even completely erased.

Since these sounds are simply "stuck" into the machine, lining them up in rhythm patterns is very easy and very fast. The user can arrange the different drums into open measures called patterns. A pattern is a memory section of the drum machine that can be programmed any way the user wants. If you want a pattern such as tom/tom/snare/bass with a cymbal over the snare, the machine allows you to punch in those drums in that pattern. It works the same way as programming a VCR to record David Letterman one night and then to skip all other TV shows until "Pee Wee's Playhouse" on Saturday morning. The VCR has buttons which let you select the date, the time of day, the channel, and the duration of the recording, even when you are not there. A drum machine works on the same principle, which is known by the fairly generic term of programmable memory. You program the machine's memory to remember the pattern or configuration you've put into it.

As with a VCR, you can program the drum machine for more than just one pattern—there are usually between 32 and 128 programmable opportunities on a standard drum machine. Each of these is then put into the machine's memory, but unlike the sounds themselves, these patterns can be changed at any time in the future.

Drum machines tend to have less variation in the types of features they have than do other kinds of synthesizers, so their functions are very similar from model to model. A typical drum machine has from 12 to 48 sounds available inside of it (Fig. 6–1). On the average, these are a snare, three fly toms, two floor toms, one kick or bass drum, an open hi-hat, a closed hi-hat, a ride cymbal, a crash cymbal, a cowbell, handclaps, and a variety of other standard percussion sounds like tambourines, rim shots, some Latin percussion, other cymbals, and other variations. Some models have specific options or additional sounds like wood blocks, triangles, and brushed drums.

Each of these sounds is accessed by a small pad which is depressed to activate the sound. Some models feature a MIDI touch-sensitive pad, which means the harder you hit the pad, the louder or more intense the sound. This is especially useful when accenting fills or rolls. But since a drummer can only use two hands on these pads—and in most cases uses only two fingers, like a hunt-and-peck typist—the manufacturers have included something special in their machines: a *sequencer.*

The most obvious example of the sequencer inside a drum machine is the number of preprogrammed patterns stored in its memory. Drum

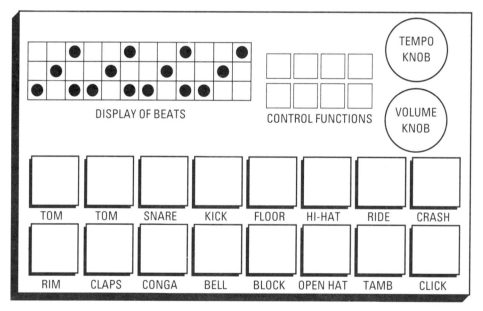

Figure 6–1. Typical drum machine format.

machines can usually store more than 80 different patterns internally, with the norm being about 96. Half of these are patterns which come pre-programmed from the factory into three different styles: some rock patterns with fills and rolls, some swing or jazz patterns, and some Latin rhythms. There are usually some less "popular" rhythms, such as a bossa nova and a reggae pattern, thrown in for good measure. When a drum machine plays a pattern, it does not store every sound in a separate pattern memory, so that you might have 96 snare sounds stored throughout memory. This would eat up your memory faster than you eat up your lunch. Instead, patterns are stored in memory by using a "map." When a pattern is played, the map tells it which drum sounds to play and in which order. This map conserves memory and allows for more pattern maps to be stored. It is a lot like a delivery system. If a delivery company had to have a delivery truck on every single street, it would be prohibitively expensive for the company to do business, because that's a lot of resources tied up all at once. Instead, the company uses fewer trucks, but each one has a map so that it can get to each street easily to deliver its goods. Drum patterns store the route to be driven, and the memory makes the appropriate stops along the way.

Since most people have their own favorite drum patterns for their own styles of music, the factory programs are seldom enough. They're fine for keeping time and practicing, but probably not for an extensive amount of performing and recording. That's why the remaining patterns are usually left unprogrammed for use by the musician.

Programming drum machines is a relatively easy process, by most programming standards. Personally, I find it harder to create patterns with the right drums than to actually punch the sounds in. In such instances, I find the help of a real drummer invaluable. I'm sure I'm not alone in thinking that drummers are the best people to program drum machines. So much for drum machines putting drummers out of work.

Most drum programming methods are divided into three parts: step editing, patterns, and songs. Each part creates the next part; a series of steps creates a pattern, a series of patterns creates a song. In the first operation, the user punches individual drum sounds into an open, or unused, pattern. This is how one gets around using two fingers to play a whole drum set. Each drum is inserted one by one into a measure, which then becomes a pattern (Fig. 6–2). Using this method, two drums can be placed in the measure at the same time, activating them simultaneously—

a snare and hi-hat, for example. Patterns are typically stored in lengths of 8 and 16 beats.

Once all the drums have been "stepped" into a pattern, they are stored as the maps I outlined above, each with its own number. These can be switched from one to the next during operation, as most machines have a buffer which lets you pick the next pattern before the present one has gone through its complete length. However, drum machines will continue to play the same pattern over and over and over unless another one is selected. Another nice feature is that each selection stays in time with the one before it.

If you don't want to hover over the machine selecting patterns after each measure, then the song feature comes into play. The song feature allows you to string different patterns together in one long-playing group of patterns as if they were part of a complete song. Indeed, this is the best way to program songs that you might be recording with other instruments later on, or even for use in live playing. A song works with patterns just as patterns worked with steps; you simply punch in the specific number of the patterns that you want to have played in the exact order that you want them played in. This provides for adding rolls before choruses, and even

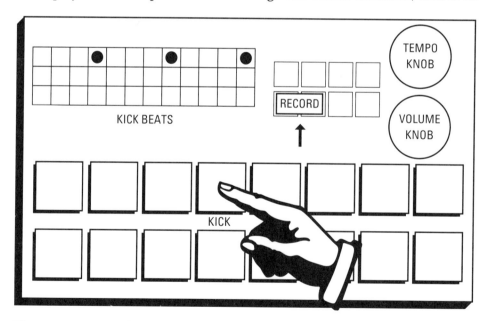

Figure 6–2. Entering drum pattern with individual drum buttons (step editing by beat).

drum solos during certain segments of the song. Of course, you have to have a good idea of what you want and when you want it to program in a whole song, but from that point on, you have the entire song stored in memory. If you program correctly, you have an untiring rhythm section at your command. And it won't make mistakes or come in a verse too early.

MIDIing Drums

The next logical step for getting the most out of a drum machine is hooking it into the rest of your setup, from MIDI connections to tape syncing (Fig. 6–3). Since drums serve first and foremost as timekeepers, a discussion of drum machine timing is essential.

Drum machines are equipped with their own internal clock, which is set by adjusting the tempo on the machine. This function allows you to set the machine's time for live performance, practice, or recording. Most machines also have a function that allows you to synchronize them to an external source, such as a tape deck or MIDI sequencer. This function, called external sync, is extremely useful if you've already laid down tracks on tape or in a sequencer and wish to add drums. Adding a drum machine to these tracks after the fact is very difficult, because if the timing is even the slightest fraction of a second off at the outset, the tracks and the drums will be way out of sync by the time the song is well underway. Since manually syncing the drums to the other machines is extremely difficult to do precisely every time, the sync function is one of the drum machine's most vital.

To sync drums to a tape, you can often use an inaudible electronic signal from the drum machine to lay down a timing track on the tape before any recording starts. This is usually done on the outside track of a tape so that it's not recorded over. This timing track contains the time code for the song, and is created by recording a specific type of timing information, usually Frequency Shift Keying (FSK) and occasionally SMPTE code. FSK puts down alternating audio frequencies—as opposed to digital signal—on a tape to provide a metronome-like guide for timing functions. SMPTE code is the universally accepted time code for the movie and TV industry, from which the term SMPTE (pronounced "simp-tee," which rhymes with "simply") comes. SMPTE stands for the Society of Motion Picture and Television Engineers, and the code breaks all information down into hours, minutes, seconds, and 1/24ths of a second. This latter

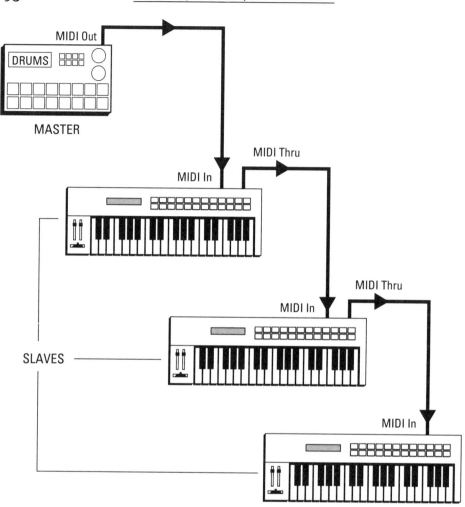

Figure 6–3. **Multiple instruments connected by MIDI (with drum machine as "master").**

number comes from the standard film speed, which is 24 frames per second. The time codes act as an electronic and inaudible click track that keeps other instruments using the same time code in sync. Ultimately, they are simply *timed electronic pulses* that mark the tape as it goes by, setting down signal marks as reference points for electronic instruments which will be recorded later. In the case of drum machines and FSK or SMPTE code, the TAPE SYNC function is selected when it comes time to record the drums, and then the drum pattern adjusts itself to the time code on the tape. Note, however, that SMPTE code is not yet used as frequently as FSK in this kind of application, so FSK is what most drum machines will recognize.

Syncing drums to MIDI is a little easier, because a MIDI sequence always puts out its own time signals, so that no prior timing data needs to be laid down. Simply selecting the MIDI SYNC function on the drum machine allows the drums to kick in as soon as a MIDI sequence begins. The MIDI clock sends out very frequent messages to other machines about its time signature and related timing changes. It also keeps track of how many pulses are in a song—and how many have already been counted off—by relying on a MIDI function known as the *song position pointer.* The position pointer, which is an inherent part of MIDI and not something you have to worry about, sends an update of where the master sequence is during the song so that other machines synced to the sequence can keep in time accordingly.

Using MIDI SYNC, a drum machine can actually record onto digital media like a sequencer in two different ways. The first is by recording a series of patterns one after another into the sequencer. The information is stored not as individual drum notes, but as a MIDI sequence which has registered the specific patterns that have been played. In this case, only program changes (or in this case, pattern changes) have been stored in memory. Thus, when played back, the sequence activates the specific patterns stored in the drum machine, not the specific drums.

If the patterns are changed, or another drum machine from another manufacturer is used with the same sequence, patterns that correspond to the program change commands will be activated. Nine times out of ten, these will be different patterns than what you originally wanted to record, so bear this in mind when switching between drum machines—or any instrument—with a sequenced recording.

The second method is to actually record the individual drum sounds as specific MIDI notes onto a sequencer track. Though this takes up a lot of memory, you are assured of getting the proper drum rolls and accents that you had desired initially. You will, however, have to make sure that the key notes assigned to each drum sound also correspond to other drum machines' drum-to-key note values. This is a lot easier than trying to match patches exactly between machines, and also allows you to edit out or add in specific drum notes at will.

Drum machines can be used to control the timing of a sequencer. The sequencer's own internal clock gets set to EXTERNAL MIDI SYNC, while the drum machine's remains on INTERNAL. Then whatever tempo the drum machine is set at determines the playback and/or recording of the sequencer (Fig. 6–4).

Drum machines have become relatively inexpensive and more natural-sounding in recent months, due primarily to the use of samples for internal sounds. For any musician not proficient on real drums, the drum machine is probably the most invaluable and inexpensive tool outside of the primary instrument. For drummers, it opens up a new world of recording and performing possibilities, limited only by the machine's memory and the drummer's imagination. Regardless of the drumming ability of the user, a drum machine is the anchor of a complete electronic musical setup.

GUITARS

Guitars present a unique problem in the brave new world of computer technology. Unlike drums and keyboards, which have a very definite on/off point, getting guitars to create sounds is a bit more complicated. When a keyboard or drum is hit, each sound is activated by a single pressure point on the instrument. In the case of a keyboard, hitting the key is an on signal, releasing it is an off signal. This is actually done on an acoustic piano by hammers striking the strings, a percussive attack. Keyboards make sounds using the same principle as that used in making drum sounds.

Drums have a very definite on point, the striking of a stick against a snare head, for instance. But drum sounds can rarely be modified or sustained after the initial strike. Unlike a guitar, which can have sound colors altered after the initial strike—by bending the note, for instance—a drum doesn't offer the same level of variation or expression in affecting the sound. Exceptions to this are percussion instruments such as timpani, which have drumheads that can be tuned after the initial strike by controlling the tautness of the drumhead with a depression pedal. But on a more basic level, the stick that hits the drum head simply activates a sound which is finished almost as soon as it begins. Thus, the on/off of a percussion instrument is similar to the keyboard; the drum stick strikes the drumhead (on), and is raised almost immediately after the strike (off).

The issue of guitars is not so simple. (When I use the term guitar, I am also including a whole category of plucked stringed instruments, including

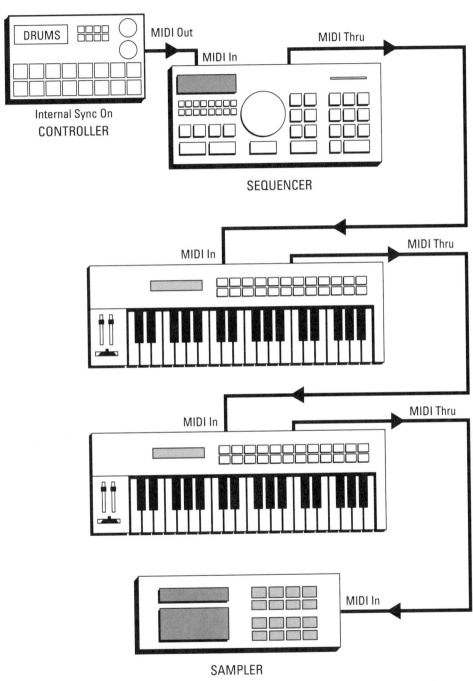

Figure 6-4. **Multiple instrument MIDI configuration; drum machine as controller; sequencer, sampler, and all synths set to external sync.**

the electric bass, 12-string guitar, banjo, mandolin, etc.) Determining the on point is easy enough—a pick or a finger plucks the string and a tone sounds. But, unlike keyboard or drum tone, the guitar tone doesn't shut off after the pluck is finished. There are a number of variables that can be employed to affect the sound before it shuts off. Whereas a drum and piano have a tone-generating surface that is fixed (the strings on the piano soundboard, and the drumhead of a percussion instrument), the guitar string can be moved after it generates a tone. As the string vibrates, it can be moved by the hand that is fretting the string. Thus, decay, sustain, and release can be controlled by the movement of the fretting finger, which can bend the pitch up and also give it tremolo.

This is only the beginning of technology's difficulties with the guitar. When you hit a drumhead or keyboard key, there is only one possible note that will emanate from that key or head at any specific point. However, the six strings of a guitar have an average of 22 different notes each that can be activated per string. Thus, the plucking of a particular string as an on function does not convey enough information to signal that a particular note is being sounded. For that information, the placement of a finger on a particular fret has to be determined. So, any string has a number of different possible notes that it can activate, while a drum or key only has one possible note value. This latter statement obviously has exceptions, notably in cases where the keyboard or drumhead had been tuned to a nonstandard or simply different tuning. But even with a tuning change, these instruments activate only one note value per event. A middle C on a keyboard is always a middle C, and nothing else (again, keeping in mind the exception of prior tuning changes). If it equals middle C when you hit it during a song, it will always equal that, and not A# or F or B♭.

Determining an exact guitar note, then, requires two different readings: the string being plucked, and the fret position of the finger. Add to this the fact that a number of strings can be struck simultaneously, and determining guitar notes seems an almost impossible task.

But it really isn't. Sure, it is quite difficult, but not impossible. Current guitar-synth methods use a few different methods of note detection to activate an electronic signal for a guitar synth. Most of the guitar synths in use today convert analog string information into digital information by using a technique known as pitch-to-MIDI conversion. This can be done with a number of different scanning mechanisms that determine at what frequency an individual string is vibrating. These include the use of light beams, radar, and digital pickups, all of which are usually mounted on a guitar body just above the bridge, and far enough from the strings to not interfere with their movement. When a string is plucked, the mechanism detects the which string has been hit, and sends that information on to a MIDI processor. Then it determines that string's movement—by means of whichever technology it is employing—and analyzes the vibration. Once it has determined the frequency of the string from its vibration—a process which usually takes about two vibrations or two frequency cycles for an accurate reading—the mechanism transmits this information in digital form back to a MIDI processor, which is usually a rack module. Here the signal is assigned the appropriate MIDI data and commands. After this is completed, the MIDI data is sent to a sound module such as a synth or sampler, or even a drum machine, in order to create something audible out of this whole process (Fig. 6–5).

This is a lot of processing and transmitting of a single signal, even when computerized modules are doing most of the work. Because of all this processing, guitar synths are notorious for a tiny amount of delay time between actual string pluck and final digital sound production. This delay affects what is known as tracking: the ability of the sound module to keep exact time with the what the guitarist is playing. Guitarists are currently stuck with this glitching in time synchronization because of all of the uncertainties involved in determining on/off data that we've discussed previously. But depending on the guitarist's style of playing, many of these glitches will not be noticeable, especially in slow, single-note runs. However, extremely fast runs, two-handed tapping, and flailing of strings with the pick hand tend to send the MIDI processor more information than it can handle, and a weird array of notes not even played may result. This is because the system is working under the weight of overload, kind of like the guy in the dam who tries to throw as many switches as possible to drain water so that the dam doesn't burst. Or maybe more like the contestants on those game shows that stand in a booth where dollar bills are being whipped around by fans. In an attempt to grab as many as possible, they usually end up with only a few dollars because they're trying to do too much at once. The guitar synth suffers the same fate under extreme circumstances. Guitarists who want to use their own instruments for MIDI controllers, though, have little choice but to employ one of these technologies on a modified standard instrument.

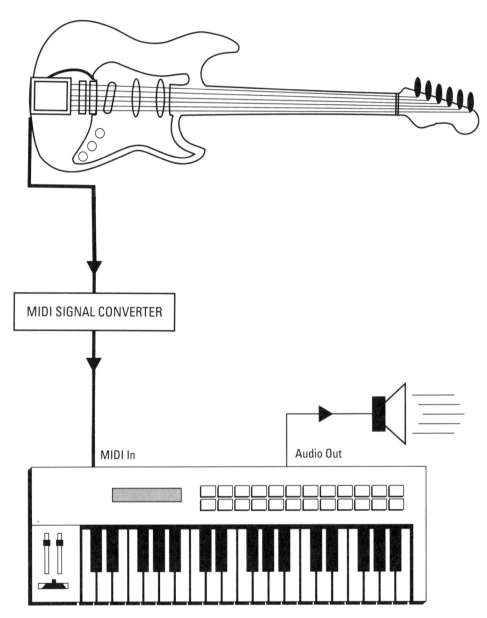

Figure 6–5.   Guitar synth using a keyboard as a sound source.

There are attempts to fix this problem, but they come at the expense of the true feeling of playing a guitar. Synth players have always complained that the synth keyboard doesn't have the correct tactile feel that makes them feel as if they were playing a properly weighted piano keyboard. Guitar players using guitar synths have this problem in spades. Another difficulty is that often the guitar becomes or is made into a controller much like a keyboard controller, which means it makes no sound of its own. This is especially strange when you strum a guitar and it makes little or no sound, or the sound it does make has no resemblance to the normal EADGBE setup found on guitars.

The makers of *dedicated guitar controllers*, which are primarily guitars used only for controlling sound modules and not for use as standalone guitars, have taken a variety of other paths. To get around the problem of determining string pluck and then note position, some of these guitars actually have the inside of the guitar neck wired with electronic sensors. This allows the guitar to determine where the finger is placed at the time the finger is placed there, even without a string being plucked. When the string is plucked, the guitar already has the information regarding fret placement, and a simultaneous signal can then be transmitted with note data.

Unfortunately, the closer dedicated guitar controllers seem to get to achieving real accuracy, the further they get from being guitars. This is especially true of the near-legendary Synth-Axe, a guitar controller which costs as much as a used Mercedes. The Synth-Axe uses two complete sets of processes for sound control. First of all, it has two sets of strings, six for the strumming and plucking hand, and six for the fretting hand. (See Fig. 6–6.) Neither set is connected. Instead they are positioned in such a way that the short strings of the strumming hand stop nearby the long strings for the fretting hand. In this way, the guitar can devote complete time to the two separate parts of playing the guitar without being concerned with trying to do both string and fret determination from one source. Unfortunately, when a player plucks the string of the Synth-Axe, his fretting hand has no feel for the resulting string movement, since the strings aren't connected. Any guitarist will tell you that this is extremely unnatural, as the two hands usually work in some kind of harmony on the same set of strings. It's like getting punched in the face and seeing somebody else feel it. Although the Synth-Axe works well, its high price tag and strange feel are large obstacles for any guitarist to overcome.

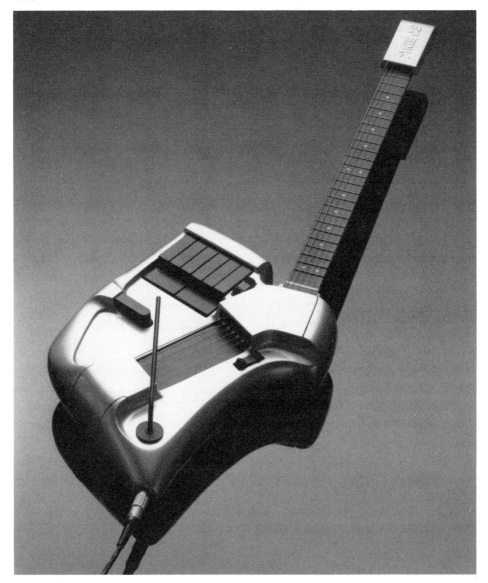

Figure 6–6. Synth-Axe.

Secondly, a guitarist must usually modify his style of playing in order to properly use a sound module. For instance, a folk-oriented strummer isn't going to get a very accurate sound by flailing away at a Flute sound. Flautists use one note at a time in performance, and attempting to recreate that sound requires the guitarist to think in the musical terms of a flautist.

While this is true of every synth player trying to mimic another instrumentalist, it is especially difficult for guitarists, who have to deal with delays in attack and phrasing caused by the limitations of guitar synths. Accessing a sharp percussive sound with a guitar synth may throw the guitarist's playing off simply because the sounds don't respond as quickly as they should because of tracking delays. Accessing any kind of sound without an immediate attack could cause the guitarist to race ahead of the sounds before they even get activated. Care needs to be taken when determining where and when to use a guitar synth.

Studio use of these instruments is pretty controllable, since the studio is a very forgiving place in terms of mistakes. Live performance is a whole other story, though. Besides the usual foul-ups that can occur in MIDI systems—too many connections, improper cabling, mixed-up patch commands, etc.—the live guitar synthesist risks playing a split second behind the rest of the band. As anyone who has ever played live knows, a split second can be enough to throw everyone into timing hell, create all sorts of havoc on stage, and provoke verbal abuse as well as fistfights. The operative phrase in this situation—at least as the technologies stand now—is "be careful."

Guitarists tend to want to have their cake and to eat it, too, especially given the singular importance of the guitar in modern music. Modifications to an existing guitar must be minimal and not affect the instrument's feel and intonation, and guitar controllers should act and feel like real guitars. This is not completely possible, but a number of compromises have been made in order to achieve a workable—not necessarily acceptable—level of digital sound control.

WIND CONTROLLERS

Traditionally left out of the discussion of digital music are those people that use their mouths to operate their instruments. While a lot of attention has been paid to keyboard players and percussionists, and only a passing amount has been dedicated to string-driven instruments, wind instruments and horns have been left out in the cold. With only a few minor exceptions, this is still basically true. But changes are being made, and MIDI horns are being blown in increasing numbers.

The problem with instruments that use air to create and regulate sound is that they are even harder to gauge and control than stringed instruments. Varying amounts of air, from short bursts to long streams, or pursed lips versus puckered lips, determine what comes out the end of a horn or wind instrument. To create a digital representation of these nuances is a computer's nightmare—or would be if it had them. At least with keyboards and stringed instruments, there is a definite on point. With the human mouth determining the on point, it can be any of a number of variations of lip shape, breath pressure, and breath flow, as well as a few others. Getting a digital readout from this very analog source is quite difficult.

Yet wind controllers are finally gaining acceptance. The control of actual notes is no problem, since most horns and winds use a fingered valve or blowhole for note selection, and these are almost as obvious in their on/off positions as keyboards are. Valve down or hole opened equals on, the reverse equals off. Easy enough. With that accomplished, all of the attention in breath-controlled instruments has been focused on the actual breath function.

The majority of today's controller instruments use a receptor/sensor in the mouthpiece (such as a diaphragm) to turn the analog movement of air into digital information—another example of pitch-to-MIDI conversion. This determines much of the attack, sustain, and decay information needed to at least provide some semblance of actual playing. Coupled with the information from the finger positions, this breath/finger combination provides the MIDI processor with the information it needs to turn a wind controller into a true digital controller. In practice, then, this works very much like a guitar synth in its pitch-to-MIDI conversion. But since horns and wind instruments are virtually monophonic as a class, there are fewer variables that need to be—or even can be—processed from the instrument. This fact makes it more like a single-string guitar synth, and cuts down on the amount of overload a MIDI processor may have to deal with.

Since these controllers are monophonic, their use is limited, but they do give wind and horn players an opportunity to create different sounds using an instrument type they feel most comfortable with. If you think about it, it's really not that much different from a decade ago, when keyboard players themselves were limited by monophonic systems. Wind controllers have nowhere to go but up (Figs. 6–7 and 6–8).

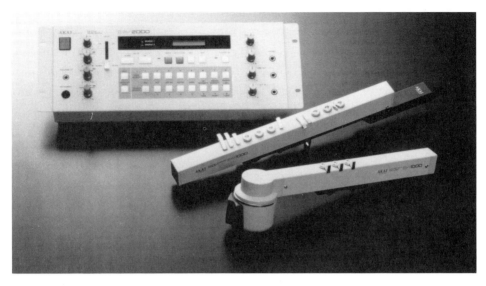

Figure 6–7.   Akai wind controllers: electronic wind instrument (left); electronic valve instrument (right).

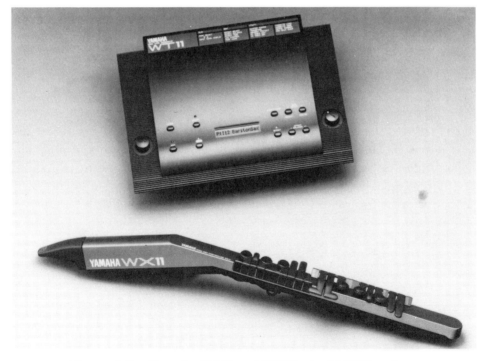

Figure 6–8.   Yamaha WXII and WTII wind MIDI system.

VOICE CONTROLLERS

Since we've touched on every other instrument type used in making modern music, we were bound to hit the human voice sooner or later. Unfortunately, there is not much to say. Vocalists have had absolutely no respect in the digital world (except when special effects and signal processors are involved), and with good reason. Look at the evolution—or de-evolution—of instrument classes that are trying to use MIDI; it gets harder with each class, starting with keyboards and working down from there. With vocalists, there are no finger positions to determine any sort of notes, or the diverse range of effects that can emanate from the human throat—from the scat singing of Ella Fitzgerald to the screams of Roger Daltrey to the Vienna Boys Choir to Italian opera to Chinese historical ballads to the cries of banshees.

Since a machine would have no better luck than most people do in deciphering vocal phrasings, all work on vocal digitization has taken the form of breath control. As we saw with dedicated wind controllers, diaphragms can be used to create digital information based on how hard air is forced into them or at them, and this information can be transformed into usable MIDI information. Right now, a few companies are developing MIDI microphones—not to be confused with Mister Microphones—which convert the moving air from a vocalist's singing into digital information for activating a sound module. MIDI microphones allow for a singer to activate another instrument patch (perhaps a bass or flute or even sampled choir) that will follow along with his or her vocal patterns, but not his actual words. Though still in its infancy, MIDI vocals will certainly become more popular as time passes, since vocalists with no instrumental ability will be able to create specific instrumental sounds, and even layer them during recording to simulate an entire band or orchestra.

7

Sampling

he most revolutionary aspect of modern music is sampling. Nothing so allows a composer or recording musician to sound more like something else—anything else—than a sampling device, or what we commonly refer to as a sampler. This is quite amazing when you realize that sampling is based on one of the oldest of music technologies: recording. A sample is a recorded sound that is then used like a patch on a synthesizer, except that now it can be a true re-creation of a speaking voice, a car crash, or a trumpet—not a computer-generated simulation or emulation.

This is oversimplifying it a bit, but not much. Sampling is a term for a specific kind of recording— recording other sounds into a form that can be used by keyboards, drum machines, guitar synths, computers, and so on. That form is *digital*, as we have already seen. Once recorded, that sound can be accessed from any of these instruments via MIDI (and in many cases, directly by the drum buttons, synth keys, or buttons on the sound module), and used as if they were normal synth sounds.

The concept is simple enough; the practice is a little more involved. Sampling is a tricky business and fairly unforgiving. Unless you have a wide selection of modification tools at hand, what you record is what you get. There are a lot of after-the-fact effects you can perform on your sample, such as playing it faster, slower, backwards, repeating certain segments, and looping it, but these are all added to the initial sample. Unlike many synthesizers, where you actually have a role in the initial creation of the sound, you don't control the elemental parameters of a sample like you do with patches. It's that inflexibility, though, that gives sampling its power of realism, and also its degree of difficulty. It's like running the most elaborate ski run on the mountain: it's hard to get all the way through it, but no other runs compare to the thrill of this one.

THE ART OF SAMPLING

As I mentioned in Chapter Two, the use of synthesis has grown from creating strange synthetic sound into creating sounds that more exactly duplicate the acoustic sounds we hear naturally. This is specifically true in using synths to replicate horns, wind instruments, percussion, and a variety of keyboard instruments ranging from cathedral organs to harpsichords and honky-tonk upright pianos. The natural evolution and development of synth technologies allowed machines to come closer to achieving these sounds with each new innovation.

But one thing synth technology has *not* been able to do is accurately reproduce sounds that have many components within a single sound (Fig. 7–1). A perfect example is the human voice. A normal speaking voice has an incredible number of different timbres, pitches, volumes, and other expressions that can be used at any given time. Think of what your voice sounds like the minute you wake up in the morning. If you're like me, even the most intelligent statement ("Good morning, honey. What's the weather forecast for today?") sounds like a constipated caveman grunting ("Gumnhnee. Tswthfcstday?"). Yet mere hours later, you are able to speak coherently, carry on conversations, sing, whisper, and even yell. Your voice is capable of all of these astounding dynamics during the course of any one day. Each of these dynamics has its own set of characteristics; for instance, whispers have low amplitude and relatively smooth timbres, whereas screaming has very high amplitudes (and decibel levels) and some pretty irritating timbres.

Even uttering something as simple as a "Hello, how are you?" carries a pretty impressive range of sound qualities that puts the tonal characteristics of a flute to shame.

Synthesizer techniques are not geared to incorporate all of these variables into a single sound. The programming aspects of trying to make additive or linear synthesis accurately mimic particular words from a human voice would drive even the most patient hardcore synthesists straight to the psycho ward.

BEGINNING
OF SOUND

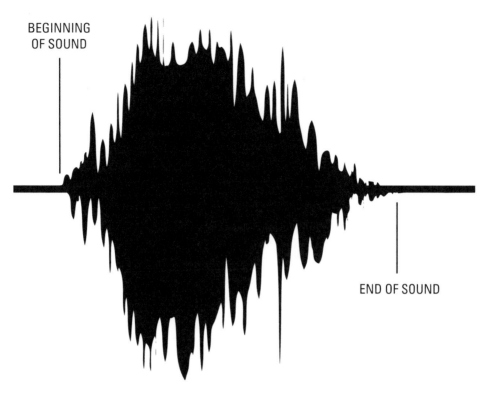

END OF SOUND

Figure 7-1. Graphic representation of one sound sample.

Yet these synthesis techniques have done an admirable job of mimicking human sounds that are much simpler than spoken sentences. Most synths do a pretty good job of emulating the "aaaahs" and "oooohs" of choir of voices, or particular voice sounds from within that choir. This is because these sounds tend to be held at a constant sound level. I don't mean amplitude or pitch, specifically, but a single, unwavering sound. It is similar to holding one note on a flute, and not adding any color to it; just simply holding one steady tone. Now, the matter would be complicated by leaps and bounds if that steady sound started to have modulation added to it. If the choir all of a sudden decided to go "ooooeeeeeeoooooaaaa," the system would have a much harder time duplicating that, because all kinds of nonconstant sound characteristics have been introduced into it. That's really an awful lot to ask from a synth that is designed to imitate the basic sound of one instrument at a time; there's just too much going on.

Unfortunately for synths, but fortunately for people, humans don't speak simply in "ooohs" and "aaaahs," except at fireworks shows. Each word, phrase, and sentence is a complicated grouping of all the varieties of sound qualities that we've just discussed. Synthesizers were not designed for such a complex task.

All of which brings us back to sampling and samplers. The best source for any particular sound is obviously the soundmaker itself. If you want something to sound like a dog barking, the best way to do it is to actually record a dog barking. This may not be too practical in a studio, and Fido may not like getting strapped down for the time that it takes you to get the right kind of yelping for your musical purposes, but that's the most accurate barking sound you're going to get—right from Fido's mouth. The same is true for the sound of breaking glass, automatic gunfire, whistling birds, roaring lions, and the whole world of natural sounds. Again, practicality rears its ugly head and says that staging a car crash in your home studio is not a very efficient way of getting a good car-crash sound. You need to be able to get these sounds without spending hundreds of thousands of dollars and perhaps endangering yourself, not to mention innocent bystanders who really aren't interested in why you're recording such strange things.

The choices so far are not particularly desirable. One requires on-location recording, the other is an attempt at getting truly realistic sounds from synthesizers which were not designed for that specific a purpose. Enter the sampler, the perfect "synthesis" of both worlds.

Let me define sampling devices before we talk about samplers in particular. Sampling devices are any kind of electronic musical equipment that use sampling as a basis for sound creation and production. The most prevalent of these instruments are known as *samplers*. Samplers are able to record and play back sampled sounds. Primarily, they are simply sound modules, which means that they need a controller of some sort to activate them. Most of them look like large and complicated cassette decks, only they record to disk instead of tape.

Next are sampling keyboards. These are keyboards that look just like synths, but they are able to record and playback sampled sounds, instead of creating their own internal sounds. They work on the same principle as samplers, only they have their own self-contained controller in the keyboard, and usually a disk drive. This type of instrument can even be found at consumer stores in the form of high-priced "toy" keyboards. These instruments, which usually cost less than $200, have a built-in microphone that allows the users to record everything from Fido growling to the baby whining and then replay that sound *in tune* on the keyboard. Unfortunately, these machines very rarely have any memory storage capability, so the sound goes away when you shut it off, and by and large have no MIDI capability. Buy at your own risk.

Then come devices which use samples burned into their memories to create sounds. These samples are not modifiable (although you can usually add reverb to them, or mix them to create new sounds), and the instruments cannot record new samples. When I say they are "burned into" memory, this means that the internal memory (and often a plug-in card with more sounds) has these samples stored in an unalterable form which was set up by the factory. The best example of this type of instrument is a drum machine, which use samples of actual percussion instruments stored in memory to create drum sounds. This type of drum machine tends to be the most accurate-sounding of the whole class of drum machines, since it is programmed using real recorded sounds.

The problem, though, with these instruments is that the original factory sounds/samples can't be easily modified. Certain effects (like reverb) can be added to them and certain values (like loudness, balance, EQ) can be adjusted, but the sounds you get in the machine are pretty much what you're going to live with. Fortunately, companies are providing a pretty realistic selection in their machines that is representative of what percussionists really need. This is good news for those musicians of the world who aren't programmers—meaning almost all of us. Getting good sounds right out of the box is a very pleasant way to work with sampled drum machines, or any kind of sample-based instrument.

SAMPLING TECHNIQUES

Sampling is the best example of the leap from analog to digital technology in the world of music. While other areas of music have grasped digital recording, nothing has reached across the line from consumer products to professional audio with such an impact as sampling.

In previous chapters, we've discussed the difference between analog and digital techniques. Suffice it to say that digital technology gives defined 1 and 0 values to analog sounds. This means that each point on an analog wave now has a specific value in terms of 1 and 0 that can now be used by computers and their microprocessors.

When you normally record a sound on your cassette deck or reel-to-reel, you're recording analog sounds with analog equipment. Then when you play it back, it's in its original form; it hasn't been altered. Analog in, analog recording, analog out. By the way, speakers are a perfect example of the *movement* of analog signals—they vibrate in order to produce sound, or the analog out.

However, computers can't process analog sounds with any degree of respectability. And since samplers are just another form of computer, something has to be done to allow them to record sounds for use in a music setup. This something is called analog-to-digital conversion, or more simply "A to D." If you look at most of the newer compact disks, they have a code on them that usually has an A to D code set in a configuration of three letters like AAD, DDD, and ADD. This is specifically used to designate the kind of input source, recording, and mastering that was done on the particular piece of recorded music. More on this later, but I point it out to show that analog-to-digital recording is becoming a rather common process.

When a sampler records an analog sound, its internal computer examines the shape of the recorded sound. In doing so, it analyzes all the components of that sound (frequencies, timbres, etc.) and assigns a digital value to each point of the sound (Fig. 7–2).

This digital value is stored in the sampler's hard memory, which is usually a floppy disk. From this point on, it can be treated as a sound patch by any instrument that accesses the sampler (Fig. 7–3). In this form, the sample pretty much resembles an internal sound on any digital synth, except that this "patch" is the real thing. If you recorded your mother saying "When are you going to get a real job?" or Mary Tyler Moore whining "Oh Robbbbbb!" from "The Dick Van Dyke Show," you can now play those phrases back by simply hitting any key on a synth that is controlling the sampler via MIDI (remember, a sampling keyboard is already hard-wired into its own sampler, and doesn't need the additional MIDI connection). Not only that, but you can get your mother to say her line for any note value on the keyboard. You can get her to say it on a low E or a high A# and any point in between. This is because the note triggers the sample at the appropriate value, just like it does with any normal patch. You hit middle C with a cello patch, the cello sounds a middle C. The same holds true for a sample. Mary Tyler Moore whines "Oh Robbbbbb!" in G# when you hit that note, or in B when you hit that one. She can even whine in chords when you depress a number of keys at once, as you normally do when

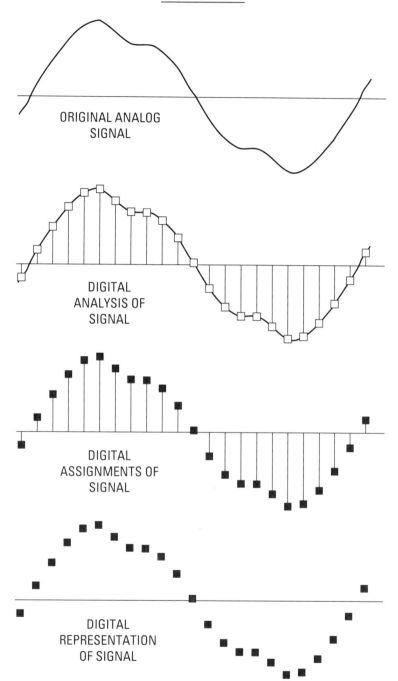

ORIGINAL ANALOG
SIGNAL

DIGITAL
ANALYSIS OF
SIGNAL

DIGITAL
ASSIGNMENTS OF
SIGNAL

DIGITAL
REPRESENTATION
OF SIGNAL

Figure 7–2. Application of digital values to an analog
signal.

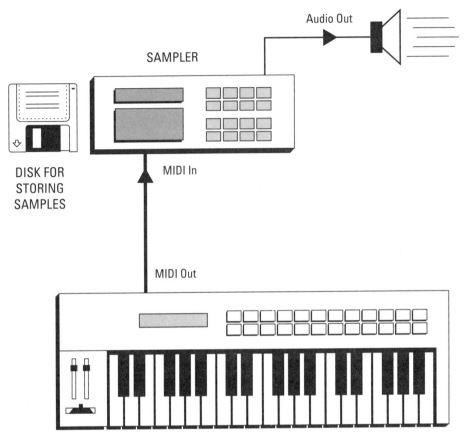

Figure 7–3. Keyboard using a sampler as a sound source.

playing music. In my experience, there may be no sadder sound on earth that Mary Tyler Moore wailing "Oh Robbbbbb!" in D minor.

You are not likely to be doing a lot of this kind of sampling for musical work, but it is good for sound effects and an occasional song highlight. An innovative example of sampling use is in the movie *Ferris Bueller's Day Off* when Ferris uses his sampler to imitate the sound of coughing his lungs out in seven different keys. To the uninitiated listener, it sounds like Ferris is actually near death. Truly a historical highlight in consumer uses for sampling.

Sampling an Instrument

In practice, a sampler is best put to use when it produces sounds exactly like other musical instruments. This is what makes sampling desirable over conventional synthesis. Probably the most difficult of these instruments is the grand piano because of all of its different timbres. Grand piano patches on normal synths are hard to come by; they often sound like spinets or heavily echoed uprights. But capturing that grand piano sound is not as easy as it may have seemed up to this point. There are lots of little nuances to sampling, and they can be difficult to deal with. We'll walk through an actual sampling session and see why.

Unlike Ferris Bueller coughing or the Three Stooges beating up on each other (which is a big favorite in most sampling libraries), your grand piano patch has to sound perfect every time you hit a note. It can't start a millisecond after you hit the key, or end before you take off your finger. You want your sample to sound like a grand piano is *actually* in the room, not some imitation. That's why you use a sample instead of some ordinary synth patch which sounds *sort of* like a grand piano.

First, you wheel your Steinway into the room where your sampler is, or take your sampler to the room where the Steinway is, which is probably easier. (We'll talk about using pre-programmed samples in a moment.)

You connect a microphone to your sampler's input, and then mike the Steinway from an appropriate place. (When sampling a sound from another electronic instrument, like a synth or electric bass, you can plug the instrument directly into the sampler using the LINE IN port, much like you do with a tape deck.) You turn on the sampler, hit a note on the piano, and then you're all set. Right? Well, not quite. At this point, you will remember that I said that samplers could be kind of inflexible. Here's why: if you started the sampler too far ahead of actually hitting the note, your sample is going to have a silent space at the front of it. This is because you have recorded the silent space as well as the note. When you hit a note on your synth using this grand piano sample, the sampler will play the silent part as well, because since *you* recorded it, it must be part of the sample. I told you that computers were dumb, and this is pretty much a prime example. The sampler doesn't know that you don't want the silence as part of your piano sample. Unless your sampler has editing features which include functions like truncating, you're going to have to do your sample again, this time without the silence.

It's very tricky to hit the piano key as soon as you hit the RECORD button, so many samplers have what is known as a TRIGGER function. This keeps the sampler from starting to record until a sound source triggers it to begin recording, much like a voice-activated recorder only starts when someone begins talking. This is because the recording device has a sensor which can detect when there is an audible incoming signal. No signal, no recording. Such a feature certainly helps the aggravating repetition of almost getting it right, not quite getting it right, and coming close to getting it right—none of which are actually *right.*

Now your sampler is ready to record only when you hit the note, so you'll be eliminating that unwanted silence at the beginning. You know you'll get the sample to start where you want it to, but you still have to make sure you get the best sample possible. That may appear obvious, but in the case of sampling you're going to have to choose which aspects of the sample are most important to you, and those two aspects are *length of sample* and *level of accuracy.* Since we're dealing with computer memory in samplers, the machine can only devote so much of its memory to a specific task. As you devote more time to level of accuracy, the length of the sampling time goes down, and vice versa. As you sample a longer sound, the process of converting each point of the sound must happen over a broader spectrum, which means that the allotted amount of "converting" has to skimp a little in order to catch the whole sound. Look at it this way. If you have one minute to read an entire ten pages of a book, you have to make a choice. You can either read as you normally do and try to get as much detailed information as you can out of the few paragraphs that you read, or you can try and skim the entire ten pages in one minute and catch as much of the entire selection as possible. One way or the other, something has to give. In the first instance, you won't have covered the complete selection, but you'll have a very accurate understanding of the first few paragraphs. In the second instance, you'll have a basic knowledge of the whole selection, but probably not a very detailed understanding of any particular passage.

Or think of it in terms of a practical musical situation—band practice. If you only have one hour to practice, do you devote half an hour of time to getting all the exact sounds and effects out of your equipment and leave only half an hour to rehearse? Or do you just plug in with little concern for the sound and get as many minutes of rehearsal in as possible? Same dilemma applies to using a sampler. If you have a long sample, like a few sentences of spoken words, then your sound quality will have to be moderately sacrificed. This means that certain frequencies—usually high ones—will be omitted in order to get the complete length of the sample into memory. This may not be noticeable to anyone but you, but a sacrifice will be made. On the other hand, a short sample of the plucked violin string will allow the sampler full memory capability to capture the entire dynamic range of the sound.

machines. In my opinion, people who sell their samples give up the right to control how they are used, pure and simple. That's a basic law of economics. General Motors doesn't get to tell you where, when, and how to drive your car after you buy it; that's your business because now you *own* it. The car was sold to you and now it's your property. The same is true of people who create samples. If they are selling them to you, you have the right as someone who has paid money for a product to use it the way you want to. (I'm skipping over the issue of software protection, which is designed for one user at a time.) In the case of samples, your music is usually heard by others if you are composing or performing. For someone to tell you that you have to pay them a royalty for their sounds because you might be making money from a sound that they created is like having Yamaha charge you for using its synthesizers on a record. If these people want control over their sounds, they shouldn't sell them.

Another part of this argument—made by those who fear samples limit true musical creation—is that using a pre-made sample will turn out a whole generation of musicians who sound like each other because they're all using the same sounds. This is like saying that everybody who buys a Les Paul guitar and a Marshall amplifier is going to sound like Jimmy Page, or all Stratocaster users will sound like Jimi Hendrix, or all Hammond B-3 players will sound like Keith Emerson. This has certainly proven to be not true; it's not the sounds or equipment that you use, it's the *way* that you use them. Every musician has the facility to shape sounds in his or her own style, and no amount of equipment and sounds—or lack thereof—should impede that. Can you imagine this kind of conversation taking place among Johann Sebastian Bach's peers when the 12-note octave was standardized? I can just imagine today's naysayers back then: "Twelve notes? Total? Are you crazy? With everybody using the same 12 notes, we'll write all the songs possible within a few years. We might as well just forget it now, because we're so limited. Are you sure we can't have more than 12?"

Then there is the issue of using sampled sounds from other recordings. Now, I'm not talking about sampling whole segments of songs and reproducing them on another recording, like the wholesale bastardization of the Led Zeppelin catalog by the Beastie Boys or the unabashed copying of all of Van Halen's "Jamie's Cryin'" for the Tone Loc rap song "Wild Thing." I'm talking only about *sounds* themselves. This part of the sampling argument is a bit stickier; actually, it's a lot stickier. It involves using samples of sounds that others have created for their own use, not for resale or public consumption. Most of this controversy began when bands started sampling Phil Collins' distinctive gated drum sound from the song "In The Air Tonight." After a few fairly slow and dirgelike verses, the drums come in with a sound that crushes your ears flat against the side of your head. Great sound, but people complained that that was Phil's unique sound. What most people don't know is that Collins *sampled* that sound from a drum machine. Yes, the sound itself is a sample. So things get confusing; is it wrong to sample a sample of something else—in this case, a drum machine?

Many musicians are known for and by the tonal qualities that they coax out of their instruments. Often this is a "trademark" sound—one that readily distinguishes them from the rest of the musicians playing the same instrument (notable examples from past and present: Charlie Parker, Eddie Van Halen, John Bonham, Jaco Pastorius, Stephane Grappelli). What happens if someone samples enough of the sounds of a performer's "trademark," and manipulates those sounds to resemble the actual playing of that musician? Well, then we get into the realm of artistic and creative ownership of that "trademark" (which also includes things like actors' and actresses' voices and likenesses, as well as catchphrases or props commonly associated with performers and artisans). The courts are still arguing over just exactly what constitutes ownership of artistic property, but it's a fairly certain bet (based on recent rulings in favor of artists like John Fogerty and Bette Midler) that very distinctive and recognizable musical traits will be protected by law in the future.

All in all, sampling of readily recognizable sounds or passages from recorded and published music is probably not a good idea. Be safe and come up with your own version of that sound by either modifying available samples or creating your own.

You can see that sampling is a pretty powerful tool in the modern arsenal of electronic musical equipment. With it, you can create truly life-like sounds that may not be at your immediate disposal in the form of the real thing. It's still one of the more expensive forms of synthesis around, and probably will be for some time. Choose wisely, and don't forget to consider the other instruments in your setup when making a decision. Things like multi-timbral capability, MIDI implementation, and ease-of-use and/or power should all be looked into carefully. Accessing the sampler with your current (or proposed) gear is going to be your biggest concern, so know what your needs, as well as handling capabilities, are. The only reason I stress this caveat more in this chapter than in others is that sampling is the most recent product technology to come down to the consumer level, it's still fairly complex, and it still costs more than most other types of equipment. A well-researched decision could keep you happy for years to come. An ill-informed one could . . . well, I shudder to think of the consequences.

8

Music
Software

oftware for music creation comes primarily in four types: sequencers, editors, librarians, and notation. Sequencers act as recording systems, editors are sound/patch/sample modifiers, librarians are storage and grouping facilities, and notation software is a form of music publishing that allows the musician to transform recorded MIDI data into complete printed scores—without ever touching pen to paper. These are very basic definitions, yet what the software does is even simpler.

SEQUENCERS

Sequencers are to the digital music world what tape decks are to the analog music world. Like tape decks, sequencers record and store music data, allowing the musician to edit that music, record multiple tracks, listen to and play back that same music, and modify it to his or her particular liking.

The difference between sequencers and tape recorders is that with sequencers, only *information* about the music is stored, not the actual music itself. As with samplers and synths, there are no sounds or notes stored in a sequencer's memory, just information about how the data is to be manipulated.

In many other respects, sequencers are exactly like tape recorders. You can do overdubs, you can fast forward, play, pause, and rewind; you have a time counter, and 8, 16, 24, 32, 64, or more available tracks. You can mute tracks, you can bounce them, you can merge them, you can sync them to other devices, and you can punch in and punch out. Though that's quite a bit of similarity, that's about where the similarity ends, because from that point forward, sequencers provide a whole new world of possibilities in both professional and home recording. They require only simple computer commands to provide these features and achieve each of these functions, and they do it with a precision not easily found on tape decks at any price.

First off, sequencers come in two forms: *dedicated hardware* and *dedicated software.* Sequencing software is usually more appealing to people than is sequencing hardware. Dedicated sequencer hardware consists of small computers which do nothing but store sequences. This is a lot like a dedicated word processor, which is nothing more than a computerized typewriter; it is not a full-function computer. Dedicated hardware sequencers can't play video games, run accounting packages, or store your Christmas card mailing list. Their purpose is only to store sequences. Using such machines in live situations is especially desirable, since the machine is dedicated only to music data, and not other applications which aren't useful or even relevant to music performance. They typically store sequences on floppy disks, as well as on internal memory.

Sequencing software, on the other hand, runs on existing IBM PCs, Apple Macintoshes, Ataris, Compaqs, clones, or any other type of hardware you can imagine. Its ability to store sequences is only limited by the amount of floppy-disk or hard-drive memory that the computer has access to. Specific sequencing software is designed for use with a specific computer, and provides a musician with all of the features of dedicated sequencing hardware. However, software is often more suitable for recording, composition, and personal use because of the large screen on personal computers, which can show more information than the small displays on dedicated sequencers. The drawback here is that few personal computers are portable; they are not easily moved, and tend to be too bulky for stage situations. This is why the smaller dedicated machines are better suited to live performance, especially when equipment has to be moved nightly or fairly frequently.

The purpose of sequencers is to store musical information for use in any musical situation, from composing to performing live. Now, let's walk through a basic sequencing operation. For our example, we'll use a software sequencer, since it not only contains all of the features of hardware sequencers, but usually has even more information available because of the nature of graphics on a computer screen. You'll see what I mean in a moment. We'll also use a multi-timbral synth in our example to show the real potential of sequencing.

In your mind and in your fingers, you have composed this wonderful orchestral rock fusion piece that requires an eight-piece orchestral group, some percussion, and maybe some straight-ahead rock sounds like electric bass or organ. This orchestral rock piece could be your ticket to the big time, but you have one minor problem: There is only one of you. Yes, you yourself, alone. All you can do is play keyboards and you don't know any cellists or oboists, let alone a decent bass player. Using normal means of composition and recording (like a band, studio musicians, or studio recording time) means that your orchestral maneuvers will probably always be in the dark. You are limited not by your imagination and talent, but by your lack of access to others who can help you create this masterwork. Your dreams of creating an incredible musical piece for the masses are dashed. In despair, you sell your keyboards and take a job as a waiter in a 24-hour downtown cafe. You know it's a ticket to nowhere. A dead-end street. A life not worth living. You leave town. Drop out of sight. The unrealized masterpiece has caused your downfall. This kind of stuff happens all the time; I must know at least a dozen people who have gone through it.

Because of technology, all is not lost; sequencers can be your salvation. Sitting down at your synth, you plug your MIDI cable from the synth OUT to your computer's IN, just as you would do if recording with a tape deck. Booting up your computer, you load in your sequencing software (Figs. 8–1, 8–2). On your screen appears a number of sections that look a lot like some of the tools you use in a recording studio: a track sheet, a counter, a metronome, the controls for a tape deck, as well as some facilities which will show you where the notes and measures are once you've recorded them (Figs. 8–3, 8–4). With a simple keystroke or mouse click, you hit the RECORD key on the screen, which is on the panel laid out just like a tape deck's (PLAY, RECORD, PAUSE, FAST FORWARD, REWIND). The computer gives an audible click to keep time, and you begin to play. As you're playing, the note information—which notes, how hard, how fast, in what order—are being transmitted to the computer over your MIDI cable. When you're finished with this first part, which you had written as a

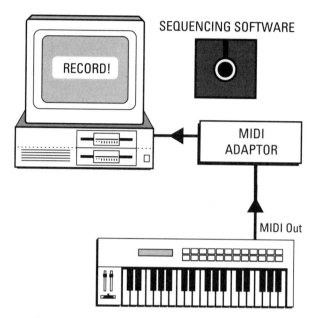

Figure 8-1.   Recording with sequencing.

keyboard part anyway—grand piano, to be specific—you stop the computer's record function.

Once you stop recording, the computer looks at all the data you've played and calculates a few very important things, like number of measures, tempo, and length of time for the piece. Depending on the software, you can then have this track displayed in one or more (and sometimes all) of the following ways:

- As an actual staff, showing note positions of what you played. In most sequencers, these notes are depicted by their physical duration, which means that instead of an actual note (dotted quarter, whole) you get varying lengths of lines showing the duration of the note.

- A track sheet showing the number of measures, and which measures actually have music in them. Each measure is often represented as a small box which is either filled in to show the presence of notes in that measure, or blank to show an absence of playing in that measure.

- An overview sheet, which shows how many tracks you've used, and which ones actually have information on them.

- An actual work sheet, exactly like the piece of paper used in recording sessions to keep track of what instruments went where. If you've ever worked with

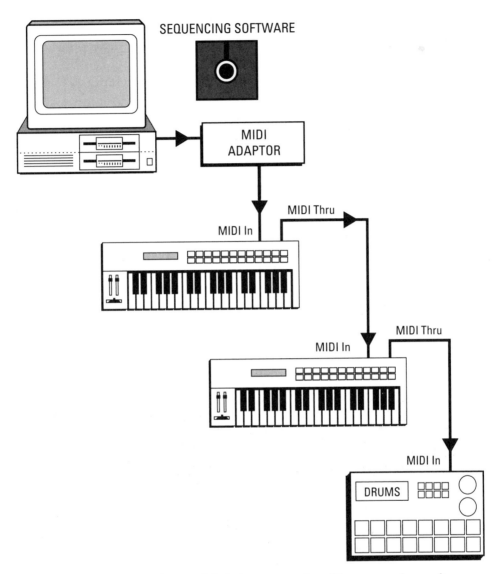

Figure 8-2. Controlling multiple instruments with sequencing software.

these sheets—and misplaced them—having them on-line at all times is very similar to total ecstasy.

Your keyboard part sounds good, but you have a few measures that sound a little rough, maybe a tad off-time, and a couple of bad notes. If you had been using tape and your timing was off, you'd have to start again and

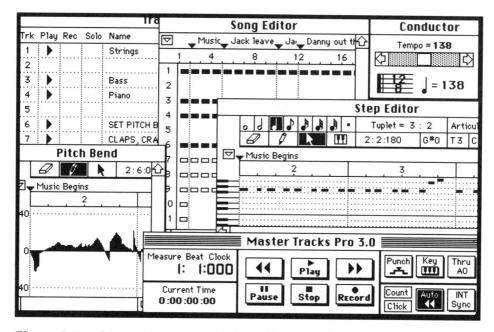

Figure 8–3. Computer screen display of Passport's Master Tracks Pro Sequencing Software.

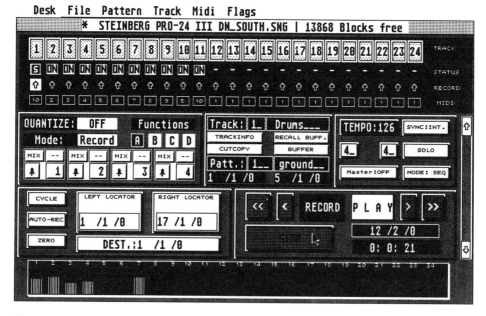

Figure 8–4. Computer screen display of the Steinberg Pro-24 III sequencing program.

play it all over. If it had just been a bad note here or there, you might have been able to selectively "punch in" the proper notes. But you've been really flailing away on this piece with some great fast runs, and you know you could never punch in those individual notes at precisely the right spots. You don't know if you could even play it the same way ever again.

With the sequencer, you can actually go in and fix those individual notes. Using your cursor, you can click a bad note and manipulate it in a number of different ways: you can move it forward or backward, you can change its duration, and you can even assign it a different pitch—making it an A# instead of an A, for instance. You can also delete notes if necessary, or insert them in the proper position if you've missed one. Each of these functions is done with the computer keyboard and mouse, and you don't need to go back to your synth at all for any of this editing. These capabilities are extremely important if you've messed up a couple of notes along the way—in any way.

Since notes stored in a sequencer are simply bits of digital information, they can be dragged from one point to another without slurring the note or causing an audible click like you get when you splice tape. This is because there is no actual sound stored, and thus it's easy to "cut and paste" this information in almost any way you want, without affecting the sound. (If I begin to sound redundant about this notes-versus-data stuff, it's only because this difference is the most important thing in understanding how sequencers work.)

Say you have got those bad notes taken care of, but you still have some measures which are obviously off-time. You can employ a feature known as *quantizing* to those measures or to the whole piece. Quantizing allows you to automatically place all notes into synchronization by moving notes so that they "drop" into precise beat positions within the measure. You can set those positions by defining how many beats per measure (including triplets), and then the computer will space the notes into correct time. Anything you may have missed timing-wise is thus shifted forward or backward—depending on whether you played ahead or behind the beat—so that all notes now fall on distinct beat divisions.

A word to the wise about quantizing: While it helps put everything back into time, there are times when you don't *want* everything to be in perfect time. This is because perfect timing sounds somewhat mechanical, or artificial, and music then loses some of its humanness. You also may not have intended for the music to be that precise in the first place anyway.

Quantizing should be employed with care, so as not to make your music sound like it was created by Robby The Robot (unless, of course, that's your intention). Some sequencers now have a feature referred to as human clocking which "re-humanizes" quantized sequences by inserting a slight off-timing into perfectly timed sequences, artificially giving the music a more natural feel.

So now you have Track One down—your keyboard or grand piano part. Since you're using a multi-timbral synth, you now select a cello patch, and record this onto the sequencer while it is playing the keyboard part back. You repeat this procedure with different patches until you've put in all your parts. Your orchestral rock fusion masterpiece is on its way to becoming reality.

Since this is an orchestral piece, many of the different parts you've written use recurring themes or repeated passages. In this case, there are shortcuts on the sequencer that you can use to save time during the sequencing process. One of the nicest sequencer shortcuts is the "cut and paste" feature. If you have a section of the score that repeats itself, or one that is used in different parts of a song or even by different instruments, then you can copy that segment and "cut" it, so that it can be moved and then "pasted" into another song area. If you don't want to repeat a very simple bass run over and over and over, you can copy it as many times as you want and put it into other places without actually having to re-record or re-play it.

Other shortcuts are simple editing features which are similar to the kinds of things you would do to when editing a reel-to-reel tape. You can insert blank measures anywhere in your score, or delete measures anywhere in it simply by specifying which measures you want deleted, or where you actually want to add more measures. This is handy when you find that you've created one part with too many or too few measures compared to the rest of your work, or that you've moved from verse to chorus too quickly or too late. A special bonus in all this editing is that since data doesn't actually move like it does on tape, there is no waiting for fast-forwarding and rewinding; you simply jump to the appropriate measure by typing it into the computer.

As you're listening to your perfect score play back, you decide that your oboe part would sound better as a clarinet. You go back into the sequencer's editing function and assign a different patch to that particular track. Now the track plays back as a clarinet instead of an oboe. You can do this kind of switching and experimenting with all of the tracks and never even have to put a single note on tape in order to test it out. In the old days, you'd have to have an oboe player play along with the other instruments, and then have a clarinetist do the same thing. Now all you have to do is click a button. This is especially useful—and economical—if you have to spend money on studio time to put this all down on tape. Even if you have your own recording facility, whether it's a home studio or just a tape deck, sequencing saves you the time and effort of having to go in and change every single track to a different sound, or sync up each track every time you add a new sound. The sequencer gives you the ability to change almost every aspect of your composition on the fly, before it ever gets put down on tape.

One big advantage of the sequencer for the home musician is how it can help you get more out of a simple cassette deck. If you're only using a cassette deck, you know that you can't get more than one recording session onto a cassette at one time. You can split it into stereo, but since a cassette deck has only one recording head, any attempt to record another track erases anything already on the tape. With a sequencer pumping out any number of tracks simultaneously (limited only by the number of timbres you have, or actual synths), then a properly rigged cassette deck can record all of those tracks almost as well as a multitrack machine—certainly a lot more cheaply, anyway. Like large multitrack decks, though, sequencers also have the ability to bounce and merge tracks (combining one or more tracks on one track, or moving one to a different track than it was originally recorded on). Again, this is done with simple commands on the computer; no re-recording necessary.

Such flexibility allows one person to become a whole band or symphony in a fraction of the time it takes to put something on tape.

Additionally, tempos can be changed during the course of a piece, as can key signatures—after you've already finished the recording. Using something commonly known as a *conductor track*, tempos can be changed at any position during the course of the song by simply inserting a new time marker in this conductor track. Conductor tracks are sort of like overview tracks that don't contain any music data, but do have control features over the whole piece—pretty much like a real conductor. As far as tempo goes, since we're dealing with digital information, all we have to is have the conductor instruct the sequencer to play the note data at a faster or slower speed.

You can also change the key of whole sections of the piece by using the conductor to indicate at what point the transposition will take place. Using the conductor, though, affects all the tracks of the piece. So if you want to change four measures of only your cello track up an octave, for instance, you don't use the conductor. Instead, you go to the cello track, specify the measures you want to change, and simply bump those measures up or down the required number of steps. This allows you to create some interesting harmonies without ever having to play the actual harmonies. Assigning the proper number of steps up or down will let you explore every possible harmony of the line that you originally played. For those that aren't particularly adept at creating multiple harmonies, this feature of sequencing is both awe-inspiring as well as somewhat educational, giving you a chance to hear how certain harmonies work—and don't work—together. It's also good for experimentation if you're not used to playing in certain keys but would like to utilize the different moods and colors found in certain keys. I've found on occasion that whole pieces sound better in a completely different key than the one I originally played it in.

Finally, sequencers provide one of the best methods for musicians involved in video scoring to synchronize music to commercials, motion pictures, TV shows, and videocassettes. Once a sequence is created via MIDI, some sequencers provide a facility for then syncing to the SMPTE time code. This code, a standard set by the Society of Motion Picture and Television Engineers many years ago, is the hour, minute, second, and frame code used for video production. It is this code that lets engineers focus on a particular frame for editing, or for adding audio effects and music. For instance, the slamming of a door has to occur in the exact frame when the door actually closes, not a frame later or earlier. Thus audio and video syncing is crucial to the illusions created on film.

SMPTE sync facilities on sequencers provide musicians with a methodology for achieving this synchronization without having to actually sit and watch the film. If the musician knows that the hideous slime-being from Planet Xenon jumps out from behind the door at 01:33:12:08 (hour 1, minute 33, second 12, and frame 8), then he or she can time the crescendo of scary music at that exact point in time, using the counter on the sequencer. This can be done in step time, which allows the musician to insert notes one at a time in order to hit that position dead-on.

LIBRARIANS

Librarians are exactly what they sound like—librarians. Instead of books, a music software librarian takes care of patches or samples and keeps them in order. It will store patch information in any order you choose, or in any arrangement you desire. If you want all your string sounds grouped together, or all your brass sounds together, the librarian lets you set it up accordingly.

There is one basic reason for using librarians. When manufacturers ship sound patches with a given piece of equipment, they usually include a fairly wide cross section of sounds, from the weird space-drool sounds to cellos and electric pianos. However, these are not always grouped in any particular order, or if they are, it might not be the way that you'd do it. Plus, as you acquire new sounds—from the manufacturer, from a third party, even ones you've programmed or developed yourself—you have a greater variety of sounds to keep track of. Trying to consult charts or remember in which bank of 64 sounds a specific patch is located could take you all day. Grouping them together in defined categories helps you keep track of what is where. This is the way libraries file books, in categories like Fiction, Nonfiction, Biography, Mystery, and so on. In music, though, your categorization is, more obviously, along the lines of Brass, Woodwinds, Plucked Instruments, Percussion, Weird Instruments, and so on.

Librarians also allow you to store more patches on a computer than your synth is normally capable of. If a standard synth can hold 128 sounds, that means that at any time it can only access the 128 sounds on board (usually split between internal memory and a memory cartridge or card). However, there are usually hundreds if not thousands of patches available for the more popular instruments, and the only alternative to plugging in a new card or loading from a tape storage device is to have a computer attached to the synth that provides immediate access to as many sounds as you may have acquired. Uploading and downloading these patches is quick and efficient with a software librarian, and it also allows you to look at what is actually going in to your synth (Fig. 8–5).

Librarians are especially useful for setting up performance samples. This is a situation where you can arrange your patches in the precise order that you will need them during a live performance. So instead of hunting all over your synth, jumping from internal patch 62 to cartridge patch 34, for example, you can order them all so that you just move to the next patch number on your synth—the desired patch has been placed there by the librarian. Even though your best cello patch may originally have been internal patch 62, and your best flute patch was external patch 12, you can now make them internal patches 1 and 2, or any other number that suits your needs.

ID	Name	ID	Name	ID	Name	ID	Name
00	*System Record*						
11	TRINI	31	SHAKUHACHI	51	PANGBORN	71	HI-HAT CLOSE
12	CEMO	32	JIMMY PAGE	52	FLUTE	72	SNARE
13	GAMELAN BELL	33	PIPE SOLO	53	PAN PIPES	73	CYMBAL RIDE
14	CELLO	34	JONNY QUEST	54	THE MACHINE	74	CYMBAL CRASH
15	VIOLA	35	CATHEDRAL	55	RAZOR GUITAR	75	CYMBAL SZZLE
16	VIOLIN	36	HAMMOND ORGN	56	GUITARKESTRA	76	CYMBAL SPLSH
17	SYNTH VIOLA	37	HAMMOND B-3	57	CLARINET	77	ARTIFICIAL
18	NATIVE DANCE	38	LESLIE ORGAN	58	ORGAN	78	INTELLIGENCE
21	SHAMUS THEME	41	THEREMIN	61	OBOE	81	*SAMPLE- 57*
22	FANTASIA	42	NOTRE	62	BASSOON	82	*SAMPLE- 58*
23	STRINGS	43	DAME	63	ALTO SAX	83	*SAMPLE- 59*
24	ARCO STRINGS	44	BRASS VOICE	64	TENOR SAX	84	*SAMPLE- 60*
25	COMB STRINGS	45	BRASS ENSMBL	65	SAX/VIOLENCE	85	*SAMPLE- 61*
26	ENS STRINGS	46	BRASS HORNS	66	SEX/VIOLINS	86	*SAMPLE- 62*
27	HORN/STRINGS	47	SAXOPHONE	67	HIGH HAT	87	*SAMPLE- 63*
28	TRINBOD	48	TRUMPETS	68	HI-HAT OPEN	88	*SAMPLE- 64*
-11	KOTO	-31	TRUMPET SOLO	-51	*SAMPLE- 97*	-71	*SAMPLE-113*

Library #1: "HPN3's Samples"

Figure 8-5. Computer library screen showing one bank of samples.

EDITORS

Most digital synths have some facility for changing some of the parameters of each patch. This usually takes the form of how much reverb is added to the patch, or changing certain points on the envelope (you remember, ADSR, and all of that), as well as things like aftertouch. Trying to do all of these fairly complicated functions on the average 4-inch-by-1-inch tiny displays on todays synths and samplers is a lot like trying to fly cross-country in a single-engine propeller plane. It can be done, but it's not necessarily all that much fun, and it might take you forever.

Editing software puts you on a 747 for your flight. Using large-screen displays on a computer, editors often show you the actual envelope, as well as the numeric values and names for other parameters, so that you can simply adjust them accordingly. The envelope graphic in most cases allows you to watch the change in the ADSR as you move the different points with a cursor or mouse. It's a lot easier to understand what you're doing when you can see it on a screen, as opposed to trying to make little push-button adjustments to numbers that represent the ADSR on your Mickey Mouse display.

Editors are usually sold with librarians, or as part of a librarian, so they work in similar ways. Patches or samples are uploaded to a computer via MIDI, and then a specific patch is selected for editing. Depending on the software, there may be dozens of individual functions of each patch that you can modify. Editors are also educational in that you can see much of what goes into creating different patches at the programming level: how different elements have been combined to create a certain type of sound, how certain sounds share certain characteristics, or even what makes a patch behave the way it does when you play it.

Once you've made changes to a patch—given it a faster decay time, perhaps—the edited patch can now be stored in place of the original, or you can give it a new name so that a new patch is actually created. Now you have two patches—the original, and the edited version, which is now its own patch with its own name. After working with editors for a while, you'll find that many third-party or after-market patches are simply modified versions of popular factory patches.

Editors for samplers, in particular, tend to be much more beneficial than on-board editing functions, simply because modifying a section of a sample is easier when you can see where that segment begins and ends, as opposed to "guesstimating" where you want to make changes based on a number table.

NOTATION

Up until just a few years ago, whenever anybody wanted to publish a piece of music, whether classical, operatic, rock, pop, country, disco—you name it—the music had to be handwritten out in a form where it could then be mass-produced in the form of sheet music. This in turn was made available to the masses through music stores and all kinds of retailers in the very readable and concise form that you find always it. But somebody had to handwrite it in the first place.

This may not seem like a big deal to many people, but there are some people to whom this makes all the difference in the world. For instance: music students who have to compose their own works and write out all the parts; symphony directors or music professors who are under contract to produce an original work for a large number of pieces; composers who must rely on studio musicians to interpret their works; musicians who score commercials, movies, TV shows, and so on; and songwriters who sell their songs to other people for performing and recording. These are all people who must handwrite music of varying lengths in order to transfer their musical ideas from themselves to others who assist in the production of those musical ideas. This does not take into consideration the many people who must deal with handwritten scores in order to interpret those ideas: musical directors of small performing groups, high schools, colleges, and theaters; studio musicians who have to read scores for recording sessions; and friends, band members and musicians for hire that must deal with handwritten scores of dubious legibility in order to assist the composer.

Suffice it to say that anyone who has to handwrite a score, and anyone who has to read a handwritten score, usually finds the process to be about as enjoyable as clumsy brain surgery. But that has been the way of the world since the first musical pieces were written out centuries ago. At that time, the transcriptions were done with so much flair and detail that they were considered as much works of art as the music being transcribed. The fact that it took months to write out a single musical work was nothing compared to the ultimate artistic value of the task. Lifetimes were spent transcribing just a few works, providing glory to the transcriber as well as the composer of the music. Ah yes, those were the days—and thank God they're gone.

Even though much of today's original music is still handwritten, it is only a matter of time before that changes completely. And MIDI is the reason why. Since MIDI is able to "tell" computers about notes being played, what their value is, what the tempo is, and divide the music into individual channels, the next logical step in this process is for computers to translate that information into notes, key signatures, time signatures, beats per measure, and specific staff and part information. That has now been accomplished through the use of music publishing software.

Barring information about patch and controller selection, almost all of the transmitted MIDI information that is created during a performance can be used to score a piece of music. Value, duration, speed, and position all have very obvious equivalents in the graphic world of scoring. It is a very simple matter to record MIDI information the way a sequencer does, and instead of putting it into a "recording studio" environment with features useful for music production, you can put the same information into a "music publishing" environment with tools specifically designed for scoring.

In most cases, notation software does a fairly simple job of "recording" a played piece using MIDI data, and converts this immediately to a picture of what was played. This picture is the staff (or staves) along with a time signature and the notes that were played (Fig. 8–6). However, this software is not all-seeing and omniscient, and more often than not requires some tweaking on the part of the composer. For instance, notes have different values in different time signatures, and the software may not always recognize this. What may be perfectly logical to the software as a double-dotted quarter note should actually be a quarter note and an eighth note in the overall timing scheme as determined by the composer. Plus, tricky playing patterns aren't always interpreted naturally by the software, so that it might not bar or tie notes across measures, or add dotted notes, to make up for the rhythmic discrepancy.

Because of this, notation software usually has a number of editing tools of its own, just as sequencing software does. The user can insert notes manually from the computer keyboard, or delete those that aren't necessary from the keyboard. In fact, an entire score can be written from the computer keyboard that can then be played back out to a synth or sound module much like a sequencer would. This kind of facility is ideal for the non-keyboard playing composer who would like to write and hear a score,

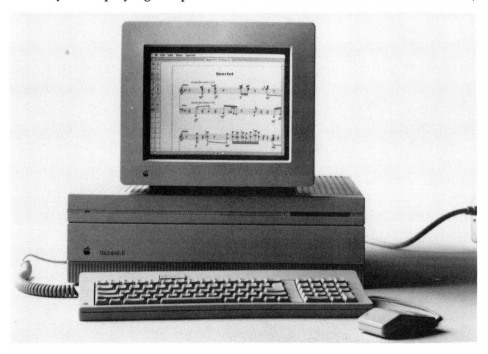

Figure 8–6. Coda notation software displayed on a Macintosh personal computer.

without actually having to play it into the software via synth keyboard. Using the computer keyboard provides the same end result, although it takes more time. Nonetheless, it's hours upon hours faster than handwriting a score, taking it to another musician or musicians, and then waiting to hear them play it back. Plus, it's so much *neater*—almost as if it were done by your second-grade penmanship teacher.

All aspects of the score are modifiable from the computer keyboard, including the addition of lyrics, if so desired. Many programs allow for at least a grand staff (bass and treble clef), while some of the more advanced ones are able to create a page containing all of the parts for a small symphony (16 staves), including a conductor track. The best part of all of this is that it can then be printed out on a computer printer (usually a laser printer for optimum results) in ready-to-publish form (Fig. 8–7). This means that when it comes out of the computer, it looks as *good* as any score you find in a music book or symphony score; sometimes it's *better*. The joy of dealing with publishable-quality scores from the very first draft of a piece is a joy that cannot be overestimated. If the scribes from centuries past had had these types of publishing programs, they might have produced even more written music for the world.

A last point to consider. Many publishing packages now read MIDI sequencer data files. This means that the software can take existing sequencer files and create a printed score directly from the files without any additional playing or musical input. This is something to keep in mind when buying a notational program, because such a facility saves an incredible amount of time, especially if the sequences are as close to perfect as possible in the composer's mind. Replaying or rekeying long sequences that already exist elsewhere is very tedious and not a whole lot of fun, especially when you feel that there must be a way to use that existing data. This feature is sure to become more popular, and thus more standard, on software in the near future.

Even if you're not big on music publishing, it's also pretty enlightening to see what the music you've created from inside your head and with your fingers looks like on a piece of paper. Plus, you don't have to wait months for some transcriber to print it up for you. You might even get inspired to use notational software to publish a music book of your own songs. It sure beats paying somebody else to do it.

Figure 8–7. Music score printed from Passport notation software.

9

Signal Processing

or even the hardiest of musicians, the thoughts conjured up by the various types of equipment known as signal processors cause them to lose sleep, to doubt their own integrity, and wonder if life is really fair after all. With terms like chorusing, reverse gated flange, sonic exciters, aural harmonizers, and 17.5-millisecond delays, there is enough techno-babble to make a grown man cry. It might as well be the "miff-muffered moof, and truffula tree seed" from a Dr. Seuss book.

All of these terms are just part of a technology known as *signal processing*. And signal processing simply refers to ways that signals are modified or interpreted. In the real world, signals can be the radar bursts detected by your radar detector (which is a signal *processor*), they can be the information transmitted via satellites, they can be voices sent out over telephone lines, they can be just about anything that relates to information being *sent*, and ultimately *received*. The most common examples of signals that all of us deal with are TV and radio signals. Both of these are instances where signals are sent into the air, and received via signal receptors such as television sets and car stereos. Like all of these items, electric and electronic instruments transmit signals to other pieces of electric equipment that interpret them. The most obvious case is the electric guitar, which sends a signal via magnetic pickup to an amplifier, which receives that signal and turns it into sound waves (courtesy of air pressure).

Along the way, though, these signals may need some modification in order to enhance them and make them more desirable. For example, your TV set is loaded with features that process signals sent from a station transmitter (that big wire tower on top of mountains and in large enclosed areas, with all the blinking red lights on it). The features that control the horizontal hold, or that control the color tint, or even the tuning knobs which produce a clearer picture, are all examples of signal processors. Adjusting these mechanisms modifies the TV signal in some way to make it better for you to watch. The same is true of adjusting the tuning on a radio, and even adjusting the bass and treble frequencies on your stereo to customize the signal (and thus the sound) to your liking.

The exact same principle is at work in the signal processors that are bombarding the musical world. And though they have scary names and gazillions of blinking lights and sliders and knobs, their function is simply to tailor the signal of an instrument before it is turned into sound. With digital technology, the signal can be processed and reprocessed more cheaply and effectively than in the days of analog devices, which deserve a mention here.

THE HISTORY

Since the days of Les Paul, the most prevalent form of signal processing has been plain old reverb. "Reverb" is short for "reverberation," and adds an artificial depth to sound, simulating the effect of the musician playing in large rooms or even large halls. This is a result of the time it takes sound to travel about in large spaces before it bounces or echoes back to your ears. What actually took place with reverb units was that the sound was delayed by passing it over a coiled wire, and this delay created a pseudo-echo effect, similar to that heard in places like Carnegie Hall, Madison Square Garden, or even the Grand Canyon.

From reverb, which was first used in the studio, signal processors have multiplied and improved. This growth has resulted from experimentation by the premier musicians of the time, and from there, signal processors have become an integral part of any music setup—from the home practice room to the concert stage. Such experimentation initially came from rock musicians around 1967 and 1968. The first group of instrumentalists to really take advantage of signal processors were electric guitarists. In the late 1960s, an incredible barrage of psychedelic, distorted, and downright nasty sounds emerged from the guitars of people like Jimi Hendrix and Jimmy Page, both of whom pioneered the use of equipment designed specifically to alter the sound of the electric guitar. Interestingly, the first of these processors was designed by a technician in the Royal Navy, who had worked on analysis of radar signals before turning his attention to music signals.

These processors were contained in a functional pedal shape for guitarists, and usually triggered by a simple on/off switch. There wasn't much fine-tuning of these particular pieces of equipment. You turned them on and let them fly. The most famous of these were the echo device and the wah-wah pedal.

Probably the most obvious analog effect used from the 1960s through the 1970s was the Maestro Echoplex. This effect was made popular by Jimmy Page on the first couple of Led Zeppelin albums, and can be heard in the solos to "Dazed and Confused" and "Whole Lotta Love." It's design was very simply—and utterly—analog in nature. A moving tape passed across three tape heads. The tape, which worked like an 8-track, passed over the heads, and depending on where one positioned the heads, the timing of the echo could be varied. But since it was analog, it was not precise, and therefore the sound contained signal information (like noise from other effects and natural hiss from guitar cables) above and below what the pickup was sending. This produced sounds just like the test pattern after a TV station shuts down for the night. Not pleasant, but unavoidable at the time. We'll see how digital signal processing changed all this.

Next came the infamous wah-wah pedal. The wah-wah can be heard to extremes on late-1960s classics like Cream's "White Room" and Hendrix's "Voodoo Child." In early wah-wahs, when the guitar signal passed through the device, the amount of "wah" was determined by how much the pedal turned an internal knob, called a potentiometer. Potentiometers are electrical regulating devices, like volume and tone controls, that control sound by increasing or decreasing the flow of electricity. On the wah-wah pedal, the further forward it goes, the more shrill the wah; the further backward, the more low-pitched and growling the wah. Rocking the pedal back and forth (heel-toe, heel-toe) rotates the knob back and forth to produce the crying effect. Again, physical movement creates the effect.

For almost a decade, these types of effects pretty much defined all of the types of signal processing. And they remained the domain of guitar players until well into the 1970s. Only when synthesizers became commonly used did the keyboard community get to experience the full spectrum of sound processors, and it has only been within the last five or six years that these same processors have been applied to percussion instruments (the Phil Collins gated snare being a typical example).

The increasing sophistication of both studio recording and live performance began to require that signal processors follow in that same parade of sophistication. It just wasn't economically feasible to record drums in an abandoned warehouse to get a decent reverb sound, or to keep pinching tape rollers to get a flanged effect. Studios needed equipment to simulate any environment right there in the booth, while performing musicians wanted greater control over their sound no matter what size bar, hotel lounge, or stadium they were playing. At the same time, musicians at all levels of playing started discovering the beauty in customizing their instruments' sounds in their *own* particular way.

Initially, many of these devices were contained in large cast-metal boxes and wooden boxes sturdy enough to contain analog equipment. With the advent of digital technology in the early 1980s, effects began to shrink down in size, just like their larger synthesizer relatives. As a result, manufacturers could put devices into smaller and smaller packages. Since size was no longer a factor, they also began stuffing more than one effect into a box. Cramming a number of devices into one package gave musicians in both studio and stage environments the opportunity to carry multiple effects with them in very portable and convenient boxes. Today, these tend to be rack modules, and manufacturers are constantly putting more and more effects into one box, with some containing as many as 100 separate effects.

As we've seen from our change from analog to digital synths, digital information is less flexible than analog information. Thus, a digital effects device needs to offer a lot of choices, so that musicians can find something that appeals to them in all of those different effects. The effects aren't always that different; it may simply be that the difference between preset 33 and preset 34 is simply the difference between a 100-millisecond delay and a 125-millisecond delay. So in order to cover a wide range of potential and desirable effects, there needs to be "something for everyone" among those dozens of preset effects.

TYPES OF SIGNAL PROCESSING

Rather than deal with the setup of any specific manufacturer's effects rack, we'll look at what all those different types of processors actually do. What follows is a description of the major types of signal processors, as well as some of the types of equipment that employ them.

Signal Delay Processing

Most effects products make use of a delayed signal to create their effects. This is true of digital delays, reverb units, and chorus devices.

Digital delay is a very fancy term for the type of signal processor that creates reverb or echo from a sound. With *reverb,* a number of ambient or random delays are applied to create a full, reverberating sound. In the case of actual timed delay, the signal is isolated and given a specific repeated and delayed signal, causing *echo* instead of reverb. In both cases, the original signal from an instrument is repeated by the device, but at a precise moment (or moments) in time after the original signal has produced a sound. For instance, if the signal is repeated at intervals of less than 125 milliseconds, there is a brightening of the sound, but almost no noticeable delay. This is because the signal is repeated close enough in time to the original so as to be almost simultaneous with—and thus pretty indistinguishable from—the original signal. But the doubling does create a brightness in the sound, because there are now multiple versions of the same signal.

Such units also let you set the rate of decay. Since naturally occurring reverb and echoes fade with time, it is necessary to make a digital signal do the same. If the signal repeated and never delayed, you would have echoes that repeated into infinity at the same loudness as the original. Thus, yelling "hello" into the Grand Canyon at the top of your lungs would result in echoes shouting back at you at the top of *their* lungs for the rest of your life. This is certainly not an appealing thought.

Once you get above 125 milliseconds, things change big time. Around 175 milliseconds, the delay becomes very noticeable, and takes on the sound of a very quick echo. This type of echo, which produces a sound similar to one you might hear in an empty garage, is called a slap-back echo because of how quickly it repeats. It's close to instantaneous, but the delay is still noticeable. As you increase the space between the original signal and the repeated signal, the effect becomes greater. This means that the delay is much more obvious, and consequently begins sounding like you are playing in bigger and bigger rooms. If you are standing by yourself in a large gymnasium, you can expect to hear echoes about every half second. If you go to Madison Square Garden when it's empty, any loud noise you make will repeat at intervals of close to one second. Going to the Grand Canyon and shouting across it on a still day can produce echoes as far apart as a couple of seconds. This is because of the distance that sound has to travel before it bounces back to your ears. When you stand on the rim of the Grand Canyon, the sound of your yelling voice has to travel to some point fairly far away until it hits something solid and then returns in the direction it came. The further it has to travel, the longer the delay and the greater the reverb.

While huge amounts of digital delay are useful more as special effects, small amounts can be used to create artificial ambience in both the studio and on stage. A good example might be a piano player recording in a studio who is getting a very flat sound from the instrument because it is in an enclosed room. Adding enough delay can create the feeling that the pianist has actually recorded the piece in a large room, or even a small hall—both of which provide warmer sounds to the piano than the flatness of a small studio.

Chorus and Harmonizer

Another form of delayed signal processing that has become very popular is the *chorus* effect. This effect creates the aural illusion that two or more instruments are playing simultaneously, with some of the natural synchronization and pitch variances that would occur if two singers or guitarists were singing or playing the exact same thing at the same time. Even when they are doing it exactly alike, their own styles cause certain variances in the two sounds. Chorus effects create the same type of variances by first slightly delaying a signal, and then by altering the pitch of the delayed signal. Since the delayed signal is repeated almost simultaneously with the original, yet with a very minor pitch change (almost imperceptible), the effect is that of two (or more) instruments playing at the same time—as part of a chorus of instruments, as it were.

Perhaps more than any other type of effect, chorusing adds depth and warm overtones to individual instruments that might otherwise sound "naked" in recording and performance situations. It is especially useful for instruments that are soloing, as it tends to fatten up their sound—especially lead guitar and lead synth lines, which can be fairly tinny and high-pitched by themselves.

Another effect similar to the chorus is the *harmonizer.* Harmonizers allow a musician to select a specific pitch change increment which will be played almost simultaneously with the original signal. Whereas a chorus utilizes a preset pitch variation with only minimal room for further adjustment, a harmonizer can play along in intervals such as thirds and fifths and octaves. This provides for a much truer "chorus" or "choir" effect, in that you have harmonies being generated with different note values, not just a minimal pitch change of each particular note. Remember, a chorus processes a signal with just enough change that it sounds like two or more people playing the same thing; a harmonizer creates a distinct signal which differs from the original, in order to sound like two or more people playing different things—namely, harmonies.

Using a harmonizer, the signal from a solo line can result in a chord if the proper intervals are chosen for creation of a triad. This is especially useful in live performance for bands that rely primarily on one singer in the studio. On stage, the singer's voice can be electronically "harmonized" during certain passages to make it sound as if he or she has background singers singing along. A harmonizer can also help create a more interesting stage sound if a band has used lots of instrument overdubs in the studio. Simply adding an octave signal to a live sound creates the impression of one more instrument.

Harmonizers are just now coming into their own, despite being available for much of the past decade. This is due to a drop in price—which used to run well into many thousands of dollars—as well as a better understanding of just what these devices do.

Phase Shifting

Phase shifting is that kind of distortion that produces a light "swooshing" or swelling effect in the sounds from your equipment. It has a very distinct up-and-down pattern, and it sounds like a sine wave looks, if that makes sense. It's a lot like putting your sound on a fairly smooth rollercoaster where you can hear the ups and downs over time. Phase shifting was very popular in the late 1960s and 1970s, notably with pop rock groups like the Byrds and the Eagles. Two especially good examples are the middle chorus to the Eagles' "Life In The Fast Lane" as well as the end of the Beatles' "I Am the Walrus." Actually, the Beatles used phasing quite a bit, starting with the *Sergeant Pepper's* album, and the effect became a staple of hippie/hallucinogenic/psychedelic/pop music. The sound it creates is reminiscent of the rolling of waves in and out, in and out, in and out. For this reason, phase shifting was, and is, usually applied lightly to music, in order to avoid the sonic equivalent of seasickness.

Phase shifting is produced by simply shifting the place in time (known as the phase) of a signal's harmonics. That's basically all there is to it. If you can picture the position of these overtones—which are like multiple funhouse images of the original—being moved slightly away from their original positions, then you have an idea of phase shifting. The displacement of the harmonics means that various parts of the frequency are out of time, or out of phase, in relation to each other. So even though you're still listening to one sound, parts of that sound are moving at different points in time, creating a swirling effect in the total sound.

Today's digital phasers are applied to everything from human voices to drums, but are used very sparingly—more as a coloration or brief effect than throughout an entire song.

Flanging

Flanging is phase shifting's violent younger brother. Flangers have a sound similar to phasers, only emphasized to an extreme degree, so that in many cases, total sound distortion results.

Flanging was first employed by recording engineers, who would process a single signal through two tape decks simultaneously and then patch them into one mixed output. If one of the tape deck's outputs to the master mix was delayed even slightly, it caused the mixed signal to be out of phase because it was created from two out-of-time results from the same signal. This effect was usually achieved intentionally by engineers, simply by pressing a thumb lightly against one of the tape reels to slow its speed down in relation to the other deck. Depending on the amount of delay, this dual signal could be out of phase enough to cancel some of the frequencies in the final mixed signal, which meant that other frequencies would be emphasized. When certain harmonics were emphasized, it could create octave and pitch variances in the signal, generating a truly bizarre sound. Again, its use was pioneered by bands like the Beatles (who revolutionized the whole idea of tape effects with producer George Martin), and further employed by art-rock and rock fusion groups like Yes, Pink Floyd, Electric Light Orchestra, and Genesis.

Flanging is a severe effect that can range from blatant phase shifting to a combination of heavy vibrato, tremolo, and chorused effects—all of these occurring simultaneously. It has almost always been employed exclusively during intros, outros, segues, or solos, as well as for the occasional one-off effect. A very cool sound, but not one to be taken in large doses.

Sound Exciters

The next big category of signal processors used by all classes of musicians are sound exciters. Called by a variety of names from aural exciters to sonic maximizers, these devices are designed to emphasize certain aspects of a signal (or signals). They do this in a number of ways.

As we've noted, sound is composed of different types of waveforms and the accompanying frequencies. Depending on the the sound source (guitars, synths, drums, vocals, etc.), the kind of sound production devices (amplifiers), signal processors, and even the type of speaker, the original sound can be distorted in a number of ways. One of the worst ways that this distortion occurs, and yet one of the most common, is in the elimination of certain frequencies from the final sound. Normally, this involves high-frequency loss, but also can affect mid-range and low frequencies depending on the sound setup.

Sound exciters are signal processors which "boost" the lost frequencies so that they are restored to their original, or perhaps higher than original, state. Depending on the manufacturer, this is done by delaying, doubling, or shifting frequencies to make them stand out when they finally make it through the speaker. It's a lot like turning the hot water tap up higher than the cold water tap to get warmer water as the final result. If you've been using the same sink for a long time, you already know after a while how much hot needs to be added to the cold in order to get the perfect amount of "warm." Exciters are like these taps—actually, more like selective filters—in that they boost the frequency within the system (the plumbing) before it comes out of the speakers (the faucet).

Exciters are also used in the recording process to restore frequencies which naturally drop out when mixing music down from master tape to final product. Anybody who has ever listened to a third- or fourth-generation tape can attest to the sound quality that is lost even when the copy isn't that far removed from the original. Exciters used in between tape-to-tape recordings can make up for some of that lost quality by selectively bumping up frequencies that have been muddied or blurred.

Like other pieces of signal processing equipment, sound exciters are extremely easy to use, and it is mostly their high cost over the years that has kept them from being widely used or even widely understood. Many require only a period of experimentation with different sounds in order to provide any musician with a great deal of "sonic value."

Distortion

Even though almost all signal processors rely on some method of distortion to produce a desired effect (even when that desired effect is a cleaner and more accurate sound), there is a class of effects that distort simply for distortion's sake. These are favored primarily by guitarists, many of whom use distortion effects to replace the dirty or nasty sounds that were lost when digital amplifiers replaced tube amps. Tube amps produced their own raunchy sound from the heat generated by the flow of electricity through vacuum tubes. The heat that was generated would build up to the point where it would distort or "dirty up" the sound passing through the amp. Such a sound became very popular with rock guitarists, but the precision of modern digital amps eliminated that heat-oriented distortion. Guitarists have had to resort to using new digital signal-processing equipment with their digital amps to get a tubelike sound. Kind of like adding two odds together to get an even.

Digital distortion devices alter the original signal by modifying the waveforms and creating fuzzy timbres. Unlike most other signal processors, distortion doesn't usually apply any sort of delay or pitch variation to the initial signal. It alters that original signal to produce something substantially different than what originally came in. Distortion is very popular with hard-rockers and heavy-metal enthusiasts, as well as with those that want to provide an edge to pop music.

Equalizers

There is probably no more abused term in the signal-processing business than equalization (EQ). "Give it more EQ, Hal." "You think we can EQ it in the final mix?" "You really should be adding some EQ to your signal." It's like EQ cures everything except the common cold, and I'm sure somebody is trying to find a way for that to happen.

Equalization is the raising and lowering of certain frequencies of a signal. In the most basic of terms, it means adjusting the treble and bass of a sound. Using equalizers gives you much more control over how much of the treble or how little of the bass actually gets adjusted. On almost every mixing board (not to mention more and more stereos, including car stereos), you'll find three frequency bands that can be adjusted above and below zero, with positions like LOW EQ −15, or LOW EQ +15. The three bands are usually divided into HI, LOW, and MIDRANGE, and larger mixing setups may have dozens of additional different frequency bandwidths that can be modified.

In the world of digital signal processing, you've probably heard the terms "graphic equalizer" and "parametric equalizer." These are just two types of specialized equalizers. A graphic equalizer adds additional fixed-frequency bands to an existing equalization setup, so it is really an add-on device for gaining more control over a wider bandwidth. Parametric equalizers also are add-on devices, but they allow the musician the flexibility to choose specific frequency ranges for modification. If bandwidths on an existing equalizer are broken down in divisions of 50 Hz, say, then you are normally limited to adjusting all the frequencies within that 50-point range (0–50, 50–100, 100–150, etc.) A parametric equalizer will allow you to get closer to the frequency you need to modify, such as 85 Hz or 90 Hz. Just to jog your memory, the lower the Hertz, the lower the frequency and the lower the tone. Low frequencies are bass, high frequencies are treble.

Once you've spent a lot of time with equalizers, you can begin to see what makes them so valuable in providing just the right tones for your sound. As we've seen, sound itself is a pretty complex mixture of frequencies and overtones, and the ability to tweak specific parts and sections of those sound components gives you that much more control over the final sound. You'll wonder how you lived with just plain old bass and treble controls for all of those years.

Compressors

The final type of signal processor we'll discuss is a class known as compressors. Unlike the other effects we've looked at, compressors don't do anything to a signal's *frequency*, like delaying, multiplying, or shifting it. Instead, compressors work on the *amplitude* of signal, or its loudness.

Why would you want to control a signal's loudness? That should be a function of the volume control. Well, if you've ever recorded something like a human voice, an electric guitar, a flute, or any other instrument that has an extreme range between the softest and loudest part of the signal, you'll understand why compressors are important. For instance, when you get an initial level on a human voice for recording, you're hoping that the singer will stay within a certain loudness or softness of that level. However, this is not always the case. If the singer should scream too loudly, it will exceed the volume boundaries you have chosen for that particular recording, and the upper end will distort badly. If the singer should choose to whisper a part that comes in way below your recording levels, you'll get a weak signal as well as all kinds of ambient noise from within the level you chose, since the singer is not occupying that level with his or her voice.

Compressors act as a kind of floor and ceiling for incoming signals to prevent either of these problems. Depending on where the compression levels are set, high-amplitude signals are "squished" a bit to make them come into the recording "room" without bumping their heads (as it were), and low signals are given a step up so that they can be at the normal ground level, or floor, of this "room." Now you have a much more even sound in terms of space; not too many outrageous or annoying peaks and valleys in the overall production. This gives a much more pleasant and consistent feel to a sound. Compressors are also useful in live situations where certain instruments tend to get overly loud during solos.

A subset of compressors is *limiters*. Limiters specifically affect the high amplitudes in that they cut out amplitudes over a certain level. The operative term here is "cut out." Instead of gently "squishing" the whole sound, limiters wait around for a very high—and unwanted—amplitude peak, and then cut it back to a certain level. Thus, the amplitude is *limited* to a certain height. Since we're talking about limiting and not adding (compressors do both), the soft signals are not affected by limiters.

These are all very straightforward devices. The names and all the blinking lights don't have to be fearsome technical assaults on your musicianship. A little bit of experimenting and a little bit of cash can get you up to speed on these machines in no time. And the benefit to your complete music system will be obvious before you can say "supercalifragilisticexpialidocious."

10

Live Performance

Performing music live—even under optimal conditions—is a very difficult task at best. If the live situation happens to be a different showplace every night, there are the obvious matters of adjusting the previous night's sound settings to tonight's sound settings. This means adapting to a different room with different acoustics and different power capabilities every time instruments are set up and sound levels are tested. For the live musician, this is the least pleasant aspect of playing, along the lines of undergoing bone marrow transplants. Even if the venue is the same every night or day, crowd size, unexpected equipment failures, and even audience (and management's) attitude will have an impact on the show.

These are the obvious disadvantages to playing music live. But when you get down to really examining the performance situation, a number of other factors affect what is and isn't done during a live show.

Let's start with a single performer, say a guitar player who also sings. With the addition of a drum machine set on a pre-programmed pattern, the most you can hope to do is a very under-orchestrated version of popular guitar-oriented songs, which by and large tend to be of the Eagles-CSNY-old Beatles variety. However, such a setup is very popular in restaurants, smaller clubs, and lounges.

The addition of a bass player rounds out the sound, allowing for certain dynamics which are found in more conventional rock and pop songs, and if the bass player sings, harmony vocals are a possibility. Two people and a drum machine approaches the power-trio days of the mid- to late-1960s. Unfortunately, in this situation, all hands are busy, so adjustments to the drum machine are impossible.

A *live* drummer actually rounds out the group to the fewest amount of people that can work together as a controllable *band*. Such configurations have given us Cream, Rush, Emerson, Lake & Palmer, the Police, and a host of others that could put on a full-scale live show without seriously deleting any of the musical parts found on a recording. Ah, but deletions there were. I say *were*, because music technology is helping to change that.

Using three as an operative number, we can explore the different areas where technology enhances the amount of music that three individuals can make in real-time, or live. Three is actually more of a common denominator; you don't usually see more than one or two people performing in a lounge, cafe, or very small club; on the other hand, the average number of musicians that take over Madison Square Garden's stage on any particular night tends to be a minimum of four, with five or six being the norm. Bruce Springsteen and his band typically perform as an eight-piece; Pink Floyd's most recent tour was made up of ten performing musicians. From the solo hotel/restaurant/club performer to the headliner at the Garden, the new technology and equipment that have been developed over the last few years have already begun to make all the difference in the world.

Why is performing live—apart from the obvious equipment and location disadvantages—so difficult? The answer is quite simple: recording. The use of more than eight recording tracks allows a musician to create so many layers of sound and so many different musical parts that the typical four-piece band can easily create a dozen or more parts to one song that play simultaneously. Ranging from harmony vocals to harmony guitars, with sound effects and individual percussion (tambourines, handclaps, bells, etc.), even the simplest recording can have all the performers doing double duty. An overwhelming case in point is the recording of Led Zeppelin's "Achilles' Last Stand" from the *Presence* album. At one point during the song, the band's only guitarist, Jimmy Page, overdubbed fourteen separate guitar parts! Clearly, this capability makes the transition to live performance somewhat complicated.

One solution has always been to hiring more musicians for the stage show than actually played on the album. Genesis and Pink Floyd, both three-piece bands for some time, have always toured with additional musicians to re-create their recorded sound live. But this is not economically feasible or even desirable for all bands. For a group like U2 to hire additional musicians for concerts would take away from the image of the band as four very capable individuals. In this day and age of appearance and image, such a thing just *wouldn't* do.

Simple Control

The obvious advantage in using technology live is the control of multiple instruments from one's own two hands and two feet. The first instruments that took advantage of a musician's feet while his or her hands were busy were bass pedals, introduced in the late 1960s and early 1970s. These pedals, the primary example of which is the Moog Taurus pedal, are based on the foot pedals used by church and concert organists over the last few centuries. A series of depressable pedals are arranged in the shape of a keyboard (with black and white keys giving way to larger dark wooden slats) that are big enough for two feet to wander over as if they were two fingers. Set to the bass register, these pedals allowed the church organist to hold on to those mind-numbingly low bass notes while still arpeggiating across the upper scales on the regular keyboard. In fact, these pedals contributed a great deal to the characteristic resonating sound of organ music heard in churches and cathedrals.

With technology running at a mad dash in the late 1960s, and the growing importance of performing rock music live, musicians began looking for ways to reproduce their sound live. In earlier years, there was not much additional thought to performing music live, because that was also the way it was performed in the studio. Throughout the 1940s, 1950s, and early 1960s, musicians simply gathered together in a recording studio and performed in a controlled "live" environment. This was true of everybody from bluesman Robert Johnson to the Glenn Miller Orchestra to the Beatles. Les Paul's practice of overdubbing and multitracking did not become standard practice until well into the 1960s (see Chapter Eleven).

Thus, it was easy to reproduce music recorded "live" in the studio in the same way "live" on stage. The exact same music was just repeated in front of larger groups of people. However, when overdubbing and multitracking became standard fare, a musician often could be heard playing two parts simultaneously on record, usually a rhythm and solo part. In the 1960s, this was usually the guitar player. In an attempt to make the band sound fuller on stage when the guitar player had to choose between one part or the other (rhythm or solo), he could tap out a bass line with his feet to add another wall of sound that made up for the missing recorded part.

This concept was expanded when the pedals were hooked up to synthesizers and could play sounds from the synthesizer instead of just bass notes. Now a guitarist or bassist or keyboardist could add another whole layer of sound with his feet—even though it was only one note at a time. Still, a wash of sound such as simulated strings behind a small band can add substantially to the listener's perception that there are actually more instruments being played.

One of the drawbacks with playing live is that once you've started, you can't stop. Unlike the studio, where you can "take it from the break after the second chorus" or some other exact point in the song, live playing requires that the song carry on *no matter what.* You forgot the chord change after the second chorus? Tough. You better fake it and hope no one notices. Sure, any other musicians playing with you are likely to beat you bloody afterwards for making such a silly mistake, but if you manage to regain your place fast enough, you can minimize the damage. Another disadvantage of playing live: mistakes don't go away. They live on into eternity and in bad memories frequently recalled by others who witnessed it. "Hey Jim, remember when we were playing live for that record company exec and you forgot the whole third verse to . . ." Adults have been known to suffer severe breakdowns from less important events.

A lot of mistakes occur when a musician has to step out of the role of musician and become technician: turning the amp up or down, switching sound settings, changing a synthesizer patch, or turning the house lights from colored spots to strobes. It's great when you can pay someone to do this for you (or better yet, get them to do it for free), but too often, musicians have to rely on their own two hands for such technical adjustments.

Using MIDI Live

The nicest thing about advances in music technology has been that musical instruments can now communicate with each other, and nowhere is that more important than onstage. It's important in the studio, but in an era where multitracking allows one person to plays dozens of instruments, that communication is not nearly as critical as it is to live performance. Musicians need all the help they can get onstage and technology certainly helps to take the edge off of that. MIDI is the prime implementation of that technology.

There are two specific pluses to using MIDI live: the amount of freedom it affords the individual performer (whether in a solo or ensemble context), and the amount of control it gives a musician over numerous instruments simultaneously. Keep this in mind through the following examples.

Let's go back to our lounge player, the guy with a guitar and a drum machine. Up until now, the drum machine drummed its pre-programmed patterns without much concern for what was going on around it. The musician starts it, gets a four-count click, and the machine is off and running until he or she turns it off. Things change drastically, however, with the addition of MIDI.

The musician has a synth or a sampler and decides to hook it up to the drum machine via MIDI to flesh out the sound of his performance. Since the drum machine sets the tempo and the musician's hands are busy playing guitar, he uses the drum machine as his controller. This means that the machine is now presiding over the performance and will signal the synth/sampler when to act. For every cymbal hit on the drum machine, he wants to add the sound of a bell. He sets the cymbal to transmit on MIDI Channel 4, while setting the other drums in his pattern to not send any messages at all. He also sets his synth/sampler to receive on Channel 4. In this case, the cymbal actually activates A4, or the A above middle C. Thus every time the drum machine pattern hits the cymbal, it signals the corresponding A key on the synth/sampler. The sound comes from the synth/sampler without the musician even having to touch it, or even look at it (Fig. 10–1).

It can get more intricate. He can set the snare drum to activate a cello sound, or the tom-tom to activate a violin. This can get messy if every drum hit activates a different note, but not if the proper guides are put in place (Fig. 10–2).

If the musician is using a sampler, different samples can be activated by certain drums. Say there's a nifty little vocal fill he'd like to have at the beginning of each chorus that was recorded as a single sample by a female vocalist. Instead of having it activated by a regularly occurring drum such as a snare, bass drum, or hi-hat, he could program a tambourine or handclap to sound at the proper point in the song. Then, by aligning the

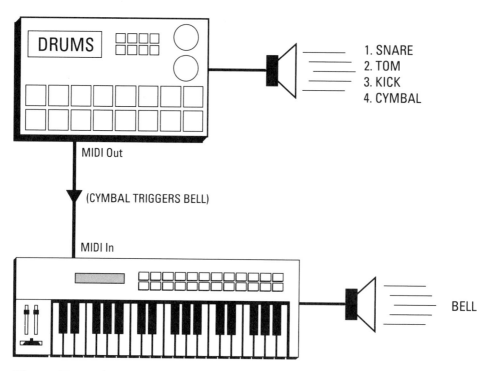

Figure 10–1. Accenting a specific drum sound with a sound from a multi-timbral synth, via MIDI.

tambourine with the note equivalent and proper channel of that sample, he could activate it only at predetermined times. When the tambourine comes in at the beginning of the chorus, so does the sampled female voice—in perfect time.

The reason for being able to perform with the above setup involves synchronization. Synchronization, as you may or may not know, is the perfectly timed performance of two or more *things*. I say *things* because synchronization can involve people, animals, machines, and almost

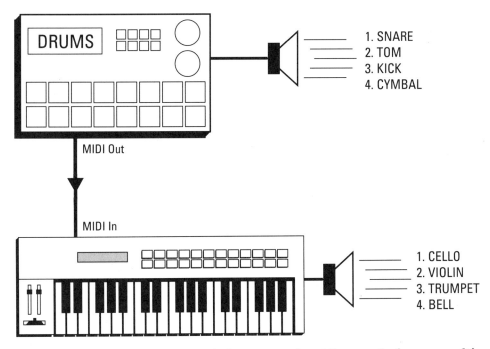

Figure 10–2. Accenting several drum sounds with sounds from a multitimbral synth, via MIDI.

any*thing* else you can imagine. There are lots of examples all around of synchronized events: pistons in an engine; those swimmers that do water ballet with every arm and leg movement performed at the same time; the rhythm section of a band; most people's watches. All of these things are supposed to happen when individual events occur at the same time as something else, creating the same or similar events.

When you play along with a drum machine, you are syncing yourself to the machine. It has already established its own timing of events, and it's up to you to match those events. This is because the drum machine doesn't care about syncing to you—its business is keeping time in its own way.

In the examples which follow, we won't sync anything to the drums. We will just be activating sounds in the machine based on the touch of a particular key or strum of a particular string. Thus, it's really more of a passive sound module in this case, more like a synth or sampler. Let's work it the other way around. The guitarist now has a MIDI guitar controller. Since drums always set the tempo whether you have real ones or ones in a box, the guitar controller can hardly be used to activate the drum machine at the proper times. But, it can be used to activate certain additional drums, or synth sounds, or even a kind of background drumming.

If the drum machine is going to be used as a tempo keeper, the guitar controller can't—and shouldn't—mess with it. But say the drum machine is not set to any pre-programmed pattern. If it is left unprogrammed, it can have its individual drum sounds activated as if they were notes on a synthesizer. An E from the guitar's sixth string might trigger the kick drum, the 5th string A might trigger the low tom, and so on. While this doesn't exactly provide a continuous backing drum track, it does allow the guitarist to get a drum sound when certain notes are played on the guitar (Fig. 10–3). This is a difficult maneuver, since both strings and/or fret notes can be assigned to different drum sounds, which gives you a large number of complex settings that are activated by your style of playing, be it fingerpicking or strumming. But for a song that has changing tempos and even points where there are no drums, this methodology beats having to kick the drum machine off on silent measures. It is especially effective for fingerpicking, when each string activates a different drum in a regular pattern. Even when strumming, a forceful downstroke on the top E string that triggers a crash cymbal is a good effect that can accentuate a perform-ance (much like Simon & Garfunkel's "kicked reverb box" on "The Boxer").

The above situation is even better managed by keyboard players, who can use different fingers and different notes to get corresponding drum sounds. While the guitarist is limited to control via six strings, the solo keyboardist can actually activate drums in time with a left-hand bass pat-tern while still maintaining the integrity of the melody on the right hand. Again, this is a function of setting keyboard notes to correspond with actual drum sounds in a one-to-one ratio.

This is the most obvious example of connecting two instruments and avoiding specific MIDI commands or syncing. It's as simple as making a telephone call; one end calls and the other responds. Easy enough, but it's when you want to have three-way calling that MIDI starts to get compli-cated, as well as more powerful.

Let's go back to using the drum machine as the controller. As noted in Chapter Six, drum machines can be programmed to play entire songs—click intro, verses, fills, rolls, choruses, cymbal crescendos, and so on—using their internal memory. With this being the case, the drum machine can play an entire song much like a real drummer would, without any

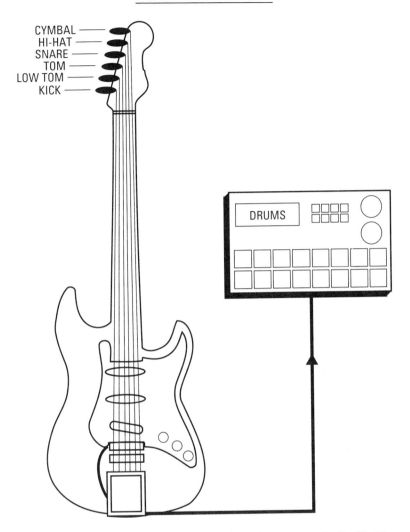

Figure 10–3. Guitar synth activating drum sounds (individual string assignments).

interference from real musicians on the stage. This is due to the drum machine's internal sequencing capability. The sequences are played in a pre-programmed order, so the drum machine plays the exact same rolls and fills night after night with nary a glitch. The logical extension of this is to get something more than percussion to repeat such patterns time and time again—something like strings, horns, harpsichords, or what have you. To do this live, we bring in sequencers.

While the most versatile types of sequencers are those that are actually computer software packages, the size of your average computer system does not allow you to carry it around easily or leave it overnight in a lounge or bar. It doesn't move very well (its internal drives are extremely sensitive to movement and easily damaged by the same), and it's a little too expensive to leave out where other people might lust after it when you're not around. For this reason, dedicated hardware sequencers are just the right addition to your live musical setup. Small and very portable, hardware sequencers can go to any gig with you and not create too much worry as to internal damage.

What to do with this sequencer? Well, let's say you've written some really good horn backing to your primary keyboard part. But since you're playing keyboards, you have to forsake the idea of having horns, unless you want to employ another synthesist or a traveling horn section. Both of these are almost as appealing as a healthy dose of the measles. With a sequencer, though, you don't need other performers, you just need another sound module.

Prior to performance, you can program the sequencer with your killer horn parts, and then MIDI the sequencer to a sound module (synth, sampler, etc.) with some good trumpet, trombone, or horn-section patches. At designated times during your performance, these patches will be activated, providing you with all the background horns you may need. The versatility of a sequencer allows you to program more backing sections to the song, as well as solos and harmonies, provided you have enough sound module capability to handle it all. You've got sixteen MIDI-equipped synths? Great. You can program sixteen separate tracks to round out your sound with absolutely no trouble. You can be the Tonight Show Band, Genesis, and yourself all at the same time.

You want to make sure that all of these things are in sync with your drum machine. No problem; the sequencer can control your drum machine, or vice versa, because they are both equipped with internal clocks which can control other clock-based devices (Fig. 10–4). As far as clock-based devices go, though, you're limited to only two: drum machines and sequencers. What a coincidence! It's probably advisable to use the sequencer as the controller, since it has the capability of sending program changes and song selection information, which means you don't have to run around

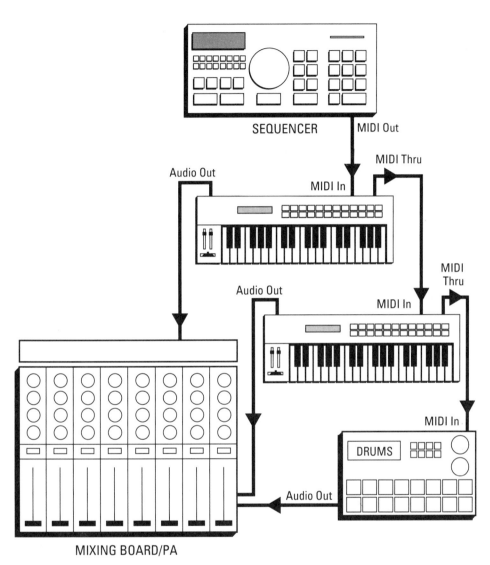

Figure 10-4. Live MIDI setup using a dedicated sequencer.

resetting your equipment between each song. A sequencer can automatically tell the drum machine which song is coming up, and when to change patterns. It can also automatically change patches on the keyboard that you are using without you ever taking your hands off of the keys. Additionally, it can send information to MIDI-controlled signal processors, adjusting your reverb or echo rates without you so much as having to blink.

I've seen performers actually leave a stage and allow sequencers to control an entire show—without one human near any equipment. Because of the ability to control patch changes as well as tempo, a sequencer can be turned on and left to "perform" an entire show, almost as if the entire show were pre-recorded, which in effect, it is. I've seen this work especially well with theatrical plays, where one keyboard player controls a multitude of sounds and instrumental parts with a sequencer. And since theatrical and bar-band budgets aren't what they used to be, getting so much mileage out of one performer is pretty fascinating, not to mention economical.

OTHER POSSIBILITIES

Just as it does in the studio, the layering of MIDI devices can produce a fuller and more interesting sound live, without your having to do anything more than connect two instruments together. A controller keyboard that accesses a number of other keyboards or sound modules really doesn't have to involve lots of program changes and system-exclusive commands, although those features are certainly advantageous in intricate systems. But even in simple linking, you can layer the sounds of different instruments to create totally new sounds, or perhaps layer the grand piano sounds of different manufacturers to get a single richer, more natural grand piano patch. For instance, I find that mixing a cathedral organ patch with a strangely ominous, low-frequency growl patch (which manufacturers or programmers usually call something like "Space Drool" or "Alien Whisper") makes an incredibly haunting sound for intros and minor-key solos. And when mixed properly, they sound like a single patch, but since it's coming from two machines, the timbres are that much thicker, with more harmonics and combined frequencies.

All of this can be further enhanced with the application of signal processors, some of which are capable of harmonizing along with live performers in real-time. This is specifically true of harmonizers. As discussed in Chapter Nine, harmonizers allow a musician to select a specific pitch-change increment which will be played at virtually the same time with the original signal. Harmonizers can play along in intervals such as thirds and fifths and octaves, creating distinct signals which differ from the original in order to sound like two or more people playing different things in harmony. Devices such as harmonizers are increasingly being equipped with MIDI capabilities, which means that they, too, can be activated by sequencers or master keyboard controllers.

Manufacturers of lighting and special effects equipment are also taking advantage of MIDI for live performance. MIDI-controlled lights—which are switched on and off, as well as to different colors, by MIDI program change—have become very important to the self-contained musical ensemble. The days of having to hit the strobe light with your right foot while turning off the blue spot with your left are almost gone, thanks to MIDI programming. All of this can be done prior to show time, and run continually, night after night, without re-programming. As all live performers know, the amount of grunt work that can be done before show time makes playing live a heck of a lot easier. With MIDI sequencers, drum machines, lighting, effects, all the homework can actually be done at home.

Essentially, building a full and clean live sound is the benefit of employing all of this MIDI technology. MIDI helps to create more instruments than there are onstage musicians, and it maintains control of those instruments at the same time. Technology has come full circle by making the one-man band a possibility again, or at least by giving one person the possibility to become a whole band.

Of course, this all takes some time, effort, practice, and most of all, experimentation. But so does preparing your skills in learning, and then performing, a song. If it was as simple as flipping a switch or turning a dial, the dorky kid down the street with the MIDI setup he got for his birthday would be staring back at you from his own album cover. Being able to get this stuff to work in phenomenal ways is what makes you a musician and him a dorky kid. *Doing it* is the only way to take advantage of the potential of live MIDI.

11

Home and Studio Recording

Recording is in many ways the ultimate product of music technology. From its humble beginnings in Thomas Edison's workshop to a multibillion dollar industry involving home music-makers and professionals in every musical field imaginable, recording is the final act of music making. It is the point at which music is captured at a specific time in history and thus preserved forever (or so we musicians hope). Live performances last only as long as the performer does, written scores are open to new interpretations by new generations of artists and conductors, and the nature of musical instrumentation itself is forever changing, usually on a month-to-month basis. Since the *invention* of recording, recording music is what establishes a musician's place in history. We have no recordings of Beethoven or Mozart, therefore, we live with their written works. Musicians, be they composers, performers, or both, have had to establish their credibility on vinyl and on tape in order to stake out any claim to longevity and (dare I say it?) greatness.

The bottom line is that recording is the *big* time when it comes to modern music. It may someday prove to be the *only* time as more and more individuals control their singular destiny with the aid of music technology, and without the aid of other musicians. Whether it's on a portable four-track recorder or a 64-track direct-to-disk machine, recording is what puts all of a musician's creative musical ideas into concrete form.

Surprisingly, while much of the technology involved in the art of recording has changed dramatically over the years—the use of signal processors, automated tape equipment, and the addition of dozens of tracks to the multitrack tape deck—the basics of recording have changed very little. Recording still involves an electronic signal emitted from a recording head arranging particles of ferrous oxide (literally, rust) on a piece of plastic tape. The electrical signal comes from a source such as a microphone and magnetically arranges the oxides into corresponding representations of that signal (Fig. 11–1). A playback head then "plays back" that arrangement through an amplification and speaker system, re-creating the original signal. Additionally, tape decks have an erase head that is used for—what else?—erasing that arrangement of particles.

This three-head configuration has remained standard throughout the history of tape recording, and is still the primary method of audio recording used around the world—even in this day and age of digital technology. This is due primarily to the billions of dollars that have been invested in analog tape recorders from the professional to the hobby level. All of this investment is not about to get chucked out the window just because digital is newer and better. It would be like having Detroit or Tokyo introduce solar-powered cars. Sure, it's a better idea: more efficient, more economical, more practical. But if you just bought a $10,000 gasoline-powered car last year, you're not about to abandon it to buy the new solar car. That's the same predicament that the recording business is in.

Digital recording is revolutionizing the process of recording, though, and will ultimately replace all analog recording equipment. Since digital technology is superior to analog technology, it is more desirable. As its price comes down in the coming years, more people will replace older, dated analog equipment with newer digital equipment. To completely replace analog will take somewhere between ten and twenty years.

I'll discuss digital recording more at the end of this chapter. There are a number of other things to talk about in terms of applying technology to existing recording methods. Much of this was initially touched on in other chapters, but we can see the true potential of all of them in a recording environment.

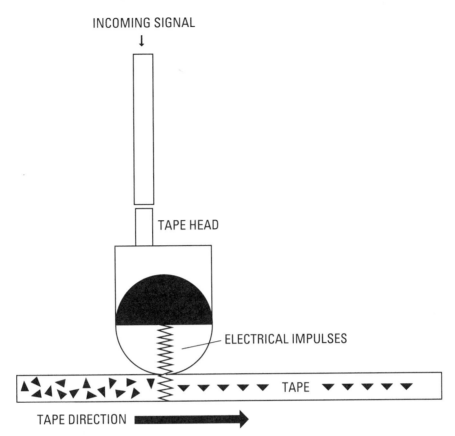

Figure 11–1. Tape head arranging ferrites on magnetic tape.

THE STUDIO SETUP

The basis for any studio, whether it's in your bedroom or in a warehouse in Los Angeles, is the tape deck. The major difference between the home studio deck and the pro deck is the number of tracks available for recording. Most home decks are cassette-based, and utilize four tracks, while pro decks are reel-to-reel-based and offer as few as eight and as many as 64 tracks (more if two decks are rigged together). The number of tracks is determined by the number of recording heads that can put information down side-by-side on one stretch of tape. Standard stereo cassette decks can only lay two tracks down side by side, but one recording head means that they have to be laid down simultaneously. Four-track cassette decks (eight-track cassette decks are also available now) allow for recording four tracks across the normal width of a cassette tape (Fig. 11–2) because they have more recording heads, but from that point on, the tapes are not suitable for listening to on standard two-track cassette equipment. Even though four-track decks use cassettes, they are "customized," once recording has begun, for use only on the four-track, and then mixed down to another tape on a standard deck for playing.

Actually, the number of tracks is not *exactly* a function of the number of tape heads, but more a function of how a tape head can be segmented and positioned over specific tracks. The principle, however, is one of multiple tape-recording heads. Another factor is the physical width of the tape itself. It's harder to cram lots of tracks on the 1/8-inch width of a cassette tape as compared to the 1- to 2-inch width of large pro-deck tape. Finally,

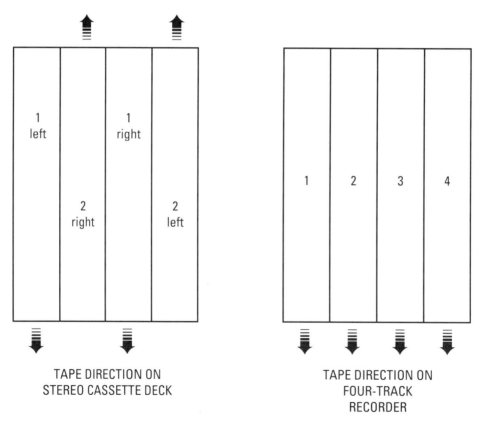

TAPE DIRECTION ON
STEREO CASSETTE DECK

TAPE DIRECTION ON
FOUR-TRACK
RECORDER

Figure 11–2. Comparative tracking configurations of stereo and four-track recorders.

clarity and quality of sound are different between these levels because of tape speed. While standard cassettes travel at a tape speed of 1⅞ inches per second, pro reel-to-reel decks can run as fast as 30 inches per second. What this translates to is more information space being used for less information. On a cassette tape, one second of music occupies 1⅞ inches of tape. By the same measure, one second of music on a pro deck occupies as much as 30 inches of tape, giving the tape more room to record a wider variety of various frequencies and overtones. It gets pretty cramped at the lower levels of tape, like trying to test-drive your new Lamborghini in the garage. Many of the four-track cassette decks can double or quadruple standard cassette-tape speed, which is a nice feature, since recording four tracks on the tape makes them unsuitable for regular stereo-deck playing anyway.

Any and every studio needs some form of recording medium such as those described above to be considered a recording studio, or a recording environment. I use the term environment because anything from a bedroom to a laundry room to a garage is capable of turning out studio-quality music these days. It's the addition of the types of equipment and technology discussed in previous chapters that makes this the case, and now we'll see how that comes about.

TIME—AND TIME AGAIN

Recording takes time. Time is the most crucial element of anybody's recording situation. This is because time is not always available, or it costs money to get that time. Recording multiple tracks takes time, setting up instruments takes time, rewinding tape takes time, re-recording botched passages takes time. It's all time. To paraphrase an old saying—time is money, money is God, therefore Time is God. While not entirely accurate, time is certainly worth its weight in gold.

Without MIDI, recording techniques would remain pretty much as they have always been: you record one track at a time (more, perhaps, if you're a band), rewind the tape after that track is done in order to record the next track, and so on and so on. To my mind, half the wasted time in a studio is due to rewinding and fast-forwarding tape. "Yeah, Bill, rewind to that part . . . no, back a little further . . . a little further . . . no, no, now you've passed it . . . ahead a little bit . . . a bit more . . . right there! . . . oh, wait . . . no, it's back a bit further . . . ." When tracks are laid down on tape, any mistake made during the performance has to be redone, requiring either a complete retake, or a punch in/punch out. For musicians with studio nerves, it can take all day to get one track down correctly, and that's a lot of time, let alone a lot of money if it's somebody else's studio.

This is because studio playing is actually a series of live performances. Each take is live, but as opposed to being live in front of an audience, you can stop and start again at any time. Part of the key to eliminating the use and abuse of time in a studio is to have all the parts done before getting ready to record. In the past, this meant practicing to the point of knowing your parts in your sleep, so that you could achieve a good take with a minimum number of attempts. That was all the homework you could do; everything else had to be done when the tape was running.

MIDI changes this homework principle drastically. With both drum machines and sequencers, you can program a number of the passages to be recorded in the studio before you ever get to the studio. The passages can also be tweaked to perfection so that you have them exactly (not just close or almost right, but *exactly*) as you want them when you walk into the studio. Whether you're using computer-based sequencing software (many pro studios now have personal computers that use a variety of sequencing packages) or a dedicated hardware sequencer, your pre-programmed sequences can be dumped straight onto tape in one blissful, complete take (Fig. 11–3).

SYNCHRONICITY

There is, however, the problem of syncing up different MIDI devices to the tape, not just to each other. Unless you want to try and dump all of the sequences into the recorder simultaneously (which can sometimes be a necessity if you only have a few tracks to play with), then you'll have to make sure that individual tracks sync up with each other. So if you put your keyboard sequences down, you want to make sure that your drum machine tracks are in perfect sync when you put them down as well. This is close to impossible if you plan on just "eyeballing" the tape to get it to start recording the new track at exactly the same point the first track was recorded. Tape stretches, counters slip, and the likelihood of getting everything in sync this way is about as likely as Richard Nixon getting re-elected President.

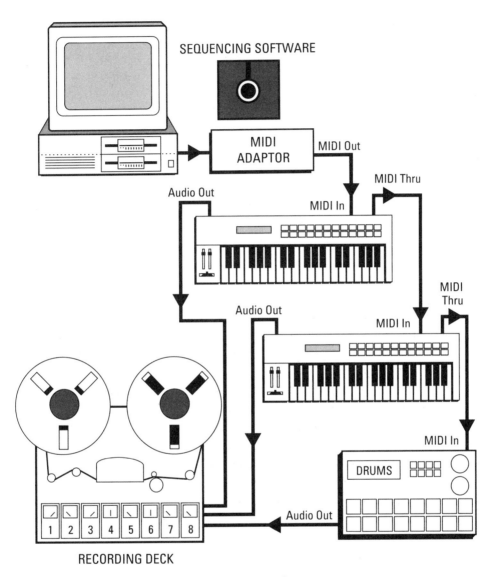

Figure 11-3.   Recording using a sequencer.

Never fear. There are a number of ways of ensuring synchronization on tape. In the past, the two most frequently used methods were pulse and Frequency Shift Keying (FSK) coding. Both of these methods utilized the process of recording a square-wave signal onto an empty track of the tape. The square wave pulses at a certain frequency—or time—and indicates to other devices the rate of speed it is operating at. FSK is a more streamlined version of pulse coding that utilizes the output of two frequencies to keep time like a metronome (shifting the two frequencies back and forth). Once either of these codes is put down on a tape, it generates a signal indicating the tempo of the recording unit whenever it is played back. This information is used to control other time-based devices (such as sequencers and drum machines) and keep them in sync.

Unfortunately, all that these coding methods can do is *keep* time, not *tell* time. It's the difference between someone counting seconds (1 . . . 2 . . . 3 . . . 4 . . .) and someone telling you *which* seconds they are counting ("It's 1:16 and 53 seconds, 54 seconds, 55 seconds . . .). The first instance gives you no indication of a precise point in time in relation to other points in time. Pulse and FSK coding are only capable of doing this type of counting, so machines that need to be synced *always* need to be synced from the beginning of the tape.

With the introduction of a MIDI clock signal and the MIDI song-pointer feature, you have a system that provides time information in the way described in the second situation—telling other devices which points in time that it is counting. MIDI clock signals, though, like all MIDI data, are digital, and tape is analog (I hope everybody has learned this by now). Thus, a MIDI clock signal has to be converted into either pulse or FSK, which requires a special signal converter.

Now we have three methods for syncing our sequencer machines to the tape. But what if our audio tape ultimately needs to be synced to video tape? Won't this make all of our initial syncing worthless in the long run? Not at all. In discussions elsewhere in this book on the standard Society of Motion Picture and Television Engineers (SMPTE) code, we've seen that all video and film recording adheres to an hour/minute/second/frame timing procedure. One of the reasons for the creation of the SMPTE standard was to isolate specific film frames for editing and adding sound effects to, as well as for more precise music scoring. To allow users of MIDI equipment to sync with this universal code, the MIDI Time Code (MTC) was created. It, too, breaks events down into hours through frames, and therefore has a strong resemblance to SMPTE. With such a close similarity, conversion is no problem, and MTC gives the scoring and sound-effects musician the ability to address video requirements much as video engineers do. Since music is usually secondary to video in the case of scoring (maybe even in the case of MTV), it is wise to follow the time code of the film.

Digital Enhancement

Now we have all these machines that can synchronize with each other on recording tape, as well as with each other in a MIDI-constructed system. However, if the amount of MIDI equipment gets too great, you run into a major dilemma: you run out of MIDI ports used to connect all of this stuff together. All MIDI instruments have a MIDI IN and a MIDI OUT, many (but not all) have a MIDI THRU port, but very few have more than any one of these. The MPU-401 MIDI adapter for the IBM PC has two MIDI OUTs for controlling more than one instrument, but that's it. Without more MIDI OUTs, you have to plug all the instruments into a line using the MIDI THRU ports. Once you hit a machine that isn't equipped with a MIDI THRU port, you're at the end of the line.

In addition, stringing this many instruments together may result in an unacceptable slowdown of the MIDI data being transmitted back and forth, which means that the instrument at the end may well be out of sync with the machines before it in no time at all.

This is remedied by the use of a number of devices designed specifically to address this problem. Known by the generic term of MIDI THRU boxes, these are just passive pieces of equipment which allow you to plug two or more MIDI OUTs into them and get six or more MIDI THRUs coming out of them. You don't need MIDI OUTs on the thru boxes because they don't generate any information on their own, they're just passing it "thru." Such devices are quite handy when you've got a sequencer controlling more than two instruments, which happens very quickly if you've got two synths and a drum machine. These devices help maintain the integrity of the MIDI signal, as well as get you by any bottlenecks that might be encountered with synths that don't have a THRU port.

Non-MIDI Equipment

There are still some things which really can't be included in this MIDI setup, like vocals and acoustic instruments, and special provisions have to be made for them. Short of very expensive analog-to-digital conversion (which we'll look at later in the chapter), these items will remain analog for some time, but they can be enhanced and manipulated by digital equipment.

While most MIDI gear can be easily regulated through the vast amount of features available from sequencers, controllers, and digital signal processors, it is only this last category that can really be applied to analog signals in the studio.

If you look back over the Chapter Nine, you'll see just how effective signal processing devices such as harmonizers, equalizers, digital delay, and related units can be when enhancing a signal. While these devices are useful in live performance, they are especially helpful in the recording environment. If you're recording in a garage, getting the right kind of ambience from a vocalist may be extremely difficult, if not impossible. Adding signal processors to the vocalist—between the microphone and the recording device—increases the possibility that you'll get a good signal worth using. Even in pro studios, such equipment provides an array of options to getting exactly the right effect and desired sound.

Microphones are still the premier example of non-MIDI equipment, and as such, tend to be one of the noisiest components in the recording environment. The use of signal processors can help to cut down on noise from microphones and assist in getting a clean sound, though the signal will not be as clean as a digital signal from a synth, drum machine, or sampler.

RACK MOUNTING

In the past, instruments were large and bulky, making transporting them difficult, and finding a place to put them even more difficult. With the advent of all the microprocessor technology that we've been talking about, all this equipment got reduced to very small components, about the size of stereo equipment. However, this meant that more and more of it could be carried around. With the addition of so many components to a stage or studio setup (most of it signal processing-based), there had to be a place to put it all.

For years, both the stereo component and video production industries have been using a fairly standardized storage system known as rack mounting. This system allows for the inserting of components into a pre-designed storage cabinet much like bakery racks and shelves—you know, like the thing they used to have in the school cafeteria that you could slide tons of lunch trays into and have them stack up on top of each other. The principle is the same with rack mounting, but instead of grungy lunch trays, you have sophisticated electronic gear. A large, open enclosure—19 inches wide—has mounting holes vertically up and down each side of the enclosure where system components can be mounted. The holes are in parallel, and regularly spaced so that different height modules can be inserted one on top of another, hence, rack mounting.

As MIDI has become more popular, it is no longer necessary to purchase an entire keyboard with keys to access different types of synth sounds. If you already have a master or controller keyboard, then you don't necessarily need the keyboard sections of other synths that you want to access. Manufacturers started building the sound modules without keyboards for just such a reason, and these modules are invariably of the rack-mount variety.

Rack-mount systems are either free-standing—designed for being used in one location, like a studio, with the components not necessarily enclosed in a three-sided cabinet—or the enclosed type that reside in an anvil or traveling case for transporting. So, when people speak of rack-mounted instruments, they are usually referring to the class of components that fit snugly into these 19-inch-wide racks. The category includes sound modules, samplers, signal processors, various effects, power amplifiers, and even tape decks in some instances.

Again, "rack mounting" refers to the packaging, not the function. Aren't you glad that's finally cleared up?

DIGITAL RECORDING

Tape recording as we know it is an analog experience, due to the way information is put down on tape. Digital recording, usually to a disk, is a digital experience, as we've seen in the case of samplers. While analog recording is limited only by the amount of tape available, digital recording is limited by two things: the power of the computer converting analog signals to digital values (known as processing power), and the amount of available memory on a hard or floppy disk. Tape is cheap; in comparison, processing power and disk memory are not. It is primarily cost that is the barrier to recording becoming an all-digital affair. The price of the computer equipment to make the analog to digital conversion, and the price of memory storage, are just too high to allow many individuals, let alone professional studios, to utilize digital recording technology.

A synopsis of how digital recording works appears in Chapter Seven. In fact, samplers are really just small digital recorders. It is the size of sampling equipment that keeps samplers from being able to actually record full tracks of music in the way that tape decks do. To give you an example of the expense involved in creating a digital recording, let me give you a very simple demonstration of digital storage.

Four filing cabinets hold a combined total of of about 40,000 documents, or pieces of paper. The average cost for a filing cabinet is about $100, so I can store 40,000 documents for about $400. Unfortunately, these four filing cabinets take up about 40 cubic feet of space in a room. On the other hand, I could store all these documents on a 40-megabyte hard disk that takes up about as much space as a box of Pop Tarts. Unfortunately, the cost of getting a hard drive this size is going to cost me double what my four filing cabinets cost. So I have to trade cost for space, and both involve some sort of sacrifice.

The same is true in digital recording. The more stuff you want on disk, the more it's going to cost you relative to tape. It's more efficient and much more desirable to record digitally since you eliminate noise, and so on, but the cost is just too great. Keep that in mind.

When analog signals are sent into a digital recording device (primarily voices and acoustic instruments), the signal is analyzed by a computer that assigns digital values of 1 and 0 to all the critical points of that signal.

To get more and more accurate signals, more values have to be assigned to more points (Fig. 11–4). This involves more computer processing power, as well as more storage space. This is directly analogous to using faster tape speeds to get more signal information. If you want more digital information per signal, you've got to provide more memory (like more tape) for that information. See how quickly our needs go up in digital recording?

With samplers, we saw how the quality of the digitally recorded signal goes down over time if you devote more memory to time than quality. In recording, you don't want to make that kind of sacrifice. You want as much time as necessary with the highest quality possible. And where we saw samplers using recording time in terms of seconds, now we're talking about continuous minutes, perhaps as much as an hour's worth. Using the kinds of samplers we looked at earlier, we'd need enough to fill Yankee

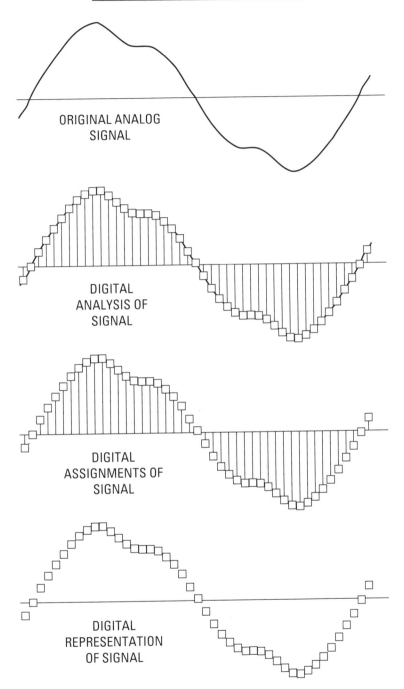

ORIGINAL ANALOG
SIGNAL

DIGITAL
ANALYSIS OF
SIGNAL

DIGITAL
ASSIGNMENTS OF
SIGNAL

DIGITAL
REPRESENTATION
OF SIGNAL

Figure 11-4.   Application of digital values to an analog signal (high resolution).

Stadium in order to get an hour's worth of decent multitrack recording. Clearly, this will not do.

Using large-scale computers much larger than PCs, we begin to approach the processing capability necessary to record an hour's worth of music. Using high-density storage devices—*not* floppy disks—we also can store that recorded information. These storage devices are hard-disk enclosures about the size of your average refrigerator, and they contain dozens of hard-disk platters for use in storing digital information. Already, we're talking a price tag in the $100,000 area, give or take (mostly give) many thousands here and there.

But remember, computers in the 1950s were the size of whole rooms, and today's pocket calculators do the same calculations in a space the size of a credit card. Both money and space came down pretty dramatically in thirty years, and eventually the same will be true for recording music.

Some bands have felt that it was worth the expense to record in a completely digital environment. Dire Straits' *Brothers in Arms,* and the Pet Shop Boys' *Actually* and *Introspective,* were all recorded directly to digital equipment. Since compact disks are quickly replacing albums in many of the homes in this country, there is a certain benefit to recording music digitally. Compact disk technology is digital technology. Completely recorded and mastered music is digitized—using the computerized conversion process we've been discussing—and then this information is cut into CDs in much the same way that grooves are cut into albums. But in the case of CDs, the grooves are replaced by microscopic dimples in the metal surface which equal 1 or 0. When a laser beam inside a compact disk player passes over these dimples, it registers the position of these 1s and 0s and sends that information back through the rest of the stereo system until it emerges as sound from loudspeakers.

So to start with digital recording means that the process can be continuous through the mastering and then the production stages. Making a CD from an analog recording requires the computerized analog-to-conversion process. And the analog recording usually has quite a bit of hiss and noise if it's an old recording, and much of this will show up on the digital compact disk. So to start recording now in digital format ensures as excellent a reproduction ten years from now as it does tomorrow.

When you pick up any CD, you'll find a three-letter code on the label which reads AAD, ADD, or DDD. This refers to the processes involved in getting the original music onto the compact disk. The literal translations of each are:

- AAD: Analog tape recorder used during session recording and subsequent mixing and/or editing. A digital deck was used for actually mastering the music—putting it down on CD.
- ADD: Analog tape recorder was used during session recording, but a digital device was used for subsequent mixing and/or editing. A digital device was also used for the final mastering.
- DDD: All aspects of the music were recorded, edited, mixed, and mastered using digital equipment.

THIS AND DAT

The reason I use the term "digital device" is because there is a new technology that has thrown a wrench into understanding the difference between digital and tape recording. It is called "digital tape recording."

You have probably heard about digital tape recording from the debate in Congress over the last couple of years about whether or not to allow the sale of digital audio tape decks, or DATs. DATs replace the disk medium commonly associated with digital recording and replace it with digital tape. Like disks, this tape has digital information printed on it; yet like analog tape, it is easily transportable and involves the passing of tape under a digital playback head. From all outward appearances these machines seem to be similar to normal decks, yet it is their use of digital technology that changes everything, because they can record music digitally! This is something that CDs cannot yet do, because of the nature of disk recording. Many record companies are concerned that people will tape CDs on DATs to reproduce digital music in an unadulterated form. With analog equipment, you get one generation of lost frequencies for every copy that you make away from the original; with digital recording there is no such loss. The information—again, in the form of 1s and 0s—transfers very easily from CD to tape.

Though DATs are aimed at the high end of the consumer market, their use is certain to spread throughout the recording business. They are already employed by some studios instead of the more costly digital disk methods, primarily in the conversion from analog mix and edit to digital master. Don't expect them to replace the home four-track for some time, though: their price of $2000+ for a consumer deck is about triple that of a decent four-track designed *specifically* for multitrack recording purposes.

While digital recording is still a buzzword in the inner sanctums of professional recording organizations, get prepared to see and hear a lot more about the technology in the next few years. It really won't have much bearing on the recording of music for at least a few years, and no major impact for almost a decade. Remember, there's already billions of dollars' worth of analog stuff out there that people aren't going to part with anytime soon. But keep your eye on digital recording; it's the next step in your evolving *digital* music setup.

12

The Future of Music Technology

The whole thrust of this book has been to look at the technology that drives the machineries of music. Each chapter has explored something related to the history, the evolution, the development, and the current use of technology in modern music. As we've seen on the previous pages, the products and the technology have been changing almost as fast as we can keep up with it. Maybe faster.

What you've read in this book covers much of music technology right up to the present day. But another question remains: what about tomorrow?

Tomorrow, indeed. If someone had asked that question ten years ago, most people would have been hard-pressed to come up with half of the stuff that exists today, especially in the digital world. There are quite a few different ideas on what tomorrow holds for the making of music; some people think that all creativity will be lost, others think that humans will create music at a rate unequaled at any time in the entire history of music. Some feel machines will take over, still others feel that machines will give even the most inexperienced of musicians a wide-open road for self-expression. Alas, the debate rages on . . . and on . . . and on . . . and on.

The idea for this book originally came out of my own interest in a computer technology known as artificial intelligence (AI). In looking at the incredible advances being made in AI (as well as its application to music), I came to realize how little material there really is on the whole subject of music technology in general. As we enter this chapter, we've come full circle, because artificial intelligence is one of the ways that music technology will move into the future.

With crystal ball in hand, tea leaves in the cup, and tarot cards on the table—not to mention my rabbit's foot, four-leaf clover, and lucky horse-shoe—I'll attempt to give you a look at what's in store for music tomorrow.

REAL MUSIC WITH ARTIFICIAL INTELLIGENCE

Artificial intelligence is a technology that attempts to make machines more human, to think and behave like humans. At places like the Massachusetts Institute of Technology, Carnegie-Mellon University, and Stanford University, researchers have been working for the last three decades to create computers which do more than simply calculate numbers. And interestingly enough, each of these universities—and others—are also leaders in the field of music technology, and right now a large amount of research is being done in the creation of intelligent machines that can make music. This is being done by creating programs that "know" how to accompany a soloist, by recognizing patterns and tempo and playing accordingly, and that can even help compose music in a specific style.

Before looking at what this research may ultimately mean to the machines of music, let's talk a little about artificial intelligence and what it really is. The term "artificial intelligence" was coined in 1957 by a group of researchers from MIT, Dartmouth, and Carnegie-Mellon. At that time, most computers were used for government purposes, doing mathematical calculations in mere hours that would normally take humans days—the kind of math problems that your basic pocket calculator can do now within seconds. The idea of smarter machines was born because these researchers believed that the room-size computers that were computing numbers could be used the same way that we use our brains; to think, to reason, to understand, to recognize patterns, to distinguish differences between various objects, and to deal with symbols and concepts as they pertain to the "real" world. The researchers came up with the name "artificial intelligence" and proceeded to work on machines that actually could do all of these humanlike things, as well as see, talk, hear, and think for themselves.

If this is your first exposure to AI, it probably seems like the beginnings of HAL 9000, the computer in *2001: A Space Odyssey,* or C3PO from *Star Wars.* Well, you're not too far off the mark, because those are exactly the kind of machines that AI researchers have been attempting to develop since day one—computers that behave like humans. Along the way, they have managed to create certain parts of this man/machine in real life: computers that can "hear" the human voice over a microphone and respond accordingly, vision systems that can "see" and are used to guide industrial robot arms, software that "understands" normal conversational phrases instead of computer jargon, and even programs called expert systems that can capture the knowledge of a specific expert on a piece of software.

When people think of such "intelligent" machines, they also get a tad frightened of the possibilities that might follow. After all, HAL destroyed the entire crew in *2001* because he . . . uh, it . . . felt that their reasoning was inferior to his. But never fear. For all of its worldly-sounding wonder, AI is still very much an infant in the world of technology. All of the things that I have mentioned above are far from being anywhere close to the capability of their human counterparts. Yes, the systems do work, but they tend to know only one thing, such as how to tell the difference between an Oreo cookie and a chocolate chip cookie, or how to repair the transmission system of a Sherman tank. Try talking to one of these systems about Mussorgsky and Stravinsky and the Beatles and Bach, or show it something that has not specifically been programmed into memory, and you will get absolutely no response. That's because AI systems tend to be idiot savants like the Dustin Hoffman character in the movie *Rain Man;* they only know a lot about one specific thing. Everything else is extremely confusing and foreign to them, and they don't know how to deal with it.

However, work is actually being done on an AI system created specifically to address the nuances of music, from theory to composition, to recording and performing. Actually, it's not one system, but many: from AI programs programmed with intelligent information about things like tempo, scales, modes, and rhythm, to programs which "know" these things so well that they are good enough to teach them to humans.

Some examples of applications are being developed which some day, in the not-too-far-distant future, may make it to your local music store. And don't think that this is just wishful techno-thinking: remember, these researchers created the world's first digital synthesizer, the DX-7.

EXPERT TUTORS

A number of universities and large computer companies are working on intelligent teaching systems that monitor music students' progress in performance as well as in theory. This is done by using a computer/synth combination to keep track of music study areas where a student does well, and where he or she shows weaknesses. Information is stored in an expert system running on a PC that also is MIDIed into a synth. If a student repeats the same kinds of mistakes over and over, the system will present new lessons to reinforce training in that particular area. Such a system is designed to provide lesson material to a student while monitoring his or her progress, and then plan changes to future lessons based on the student's capabilities at certain levels. For instance, if a problem arises in a student's ability to perform at a certain instruction level—understanding modal scales, for instance—the machine can scan through its memory of the student's performances up until that time, and may perhaps conclude that the student was prematurely given credit for having fulfilled prerequisites for the modal scales lesson, and that missing skills must be taught before going further. A new lesson is then planned by the system which will concentrate on, and help the student in, the modal problem areas.

THE INTELLIGENT MACHINE ACCOMPANIST

Work at a number of universities, as well as at some of the larger music technology companies, involves an intelligent computer "accompanist." Such a system analyzes the live performance of a soloing musician, and then plays its own accompaniment—as if it were in a live jam with the human. It does this by "listening" to and detecting changes in a human musician's playing, then adjusting its own speed and note selection accordingly. Working from more than simply a form of the MIDI "human clock" concept, the computer follows a musical score and makes its own adjustments to key signature and tempo, as well as rhythm, playing accompaniment based on where in the score—and how—the musician is playing. This is done in real-time, while the musician is actually performing. For instance, the computer may simply "listen" to the first twelve bars of a musician's playing, which it analyzes during that time. After twelve bars, the computer creates its own accompaniment on synthesizer, using a pattern it derives from analyzing the notes that the musician had played. The important thing to note here is that this is not simply a sequence which is repeated by the machine; it actually and "intelligently" develops its own accompaniment sequence for the performer's playing. This is a lot like a session musician who comes into a studio, listens to the general theme of a piece, and then adds his or her own part to the piece.

MUSICAL UNDERSTANDING

Other systems being developed around the country attempt to assist the musician in ways that a textbook can't. For instance, much of what is implicit in music, especially concepts such as style and performance techniques, cannot be gleaned from texts, and certainly not from existing symbolic musical representation (the type of notation that we have been using for centuries). Style, for instance, requires active participation on the part of the learner, and can possibly be taught and expressed in the form of computer models. Such models could be created by an intelligent system that has worked with a student and "understands" that student's strengths and weaknesses in comprehending something like style. Using artificial intelligence, systems are being designed which are interactive with the user, that explore these concepts which can't be written out in sheet music or instruction books.

As I mentioned at the start of this chapter, part of the pursuit of AI was to get machines to understand symbols and concepts, and such systems are certainly more "actively" involved in the learning process than "passive" or non-interactive textbooks are. This is because there is a great deal of similarity between research in artificial intelligence and research in music. Both involve understanding how the human mind recognizes and perceives certain symbols and patterns (signals), and then how the mind analyzes those signals and acts upon them. After all, what really goes on when we think? No one knows. What really constitutes music in an individual? No one really knows. What you think is music, your parents probably hated—no matter how old you are now. Understanding the essence and philosophy of what music is and what thought is will give researchers plenty to do for many, many years to come.

PRODUCT-IZING THE FUTURE

Before we step over that line between talking about music technology and music philosophy—it's a pretty thin line—I'll steer us back to technology. It's important to note that very little of the work described above is possible without the use of a variety of MIDI interfaces and MIDI instruments. Technology begets technology, as they say, and because of this, AI technologies and techniques are already showing up in commercial products. A number of notational software and sequencing packages use AI to recognize played patterns of music (via MIDI) and interpret them to create a notational score which is accurate by human standards. A few keyboard companies—some of which were discussed in Chapter Five—use AI to create (and in some cases, anticipate the creation of) samples and patches, as well as simple accompaniment. And these examples are only just the beginning, since both AI and digital music technology have only become firmly entrenched in the real world of products over the past five years.

As we master the power of new technologies, they will definitely show up in music products once they become efficient and economical. Unusual types of technology, notably interactive and optical-based technologies, are already showing up in the computer world, so it's only a matter of time before they show up in the music world. One technology, interactive MIDI compact disks, is creeping into some musical circles, and may change the way people listen to recorded music. Instead of getting a fully recorded and mixed disk as you do now when you buy an artist's latest work, these disks may simply contain the MIDI information that allows you to plug in synths and samplers to a highly-interactive CD player. Thus, you might control which sounds are actually being played from the score another composer has put down in what is basically a sequencer CD. You won't be able to change the score, but you'll have control of the way you want it to sound. This technology is one that is geared more to the listener, and may in fact have a negative bearing on the composer's role in the final creative process. I mention it here to give you an indication of the mind-boggling possibilities that will show up on your doorstep—or in your speakers—over the next decade.

Reading, asking questions of your local music merchants, and a willingness to learn are the best ways to prepare for this onslaught of awe-inspiring machines for making music. Sitting back and watching it pass by will assure you of a slow and probably very painful death as the world of music becomes more and more computerized. Being informed is a small price to pay for coming out on top, because the more you understand how to use the tools at your disposal, the better equipped you are to succeed in your musical endeavors—whatever they may be. I have only one piece of advice to leave you with, as we all charge into the brave new world of music:

Be ready for anything. And everything.

Index